THE AUDUBON SOCIETY

by Les Line, Kimball L. Garrett, and Kenn Kaufman

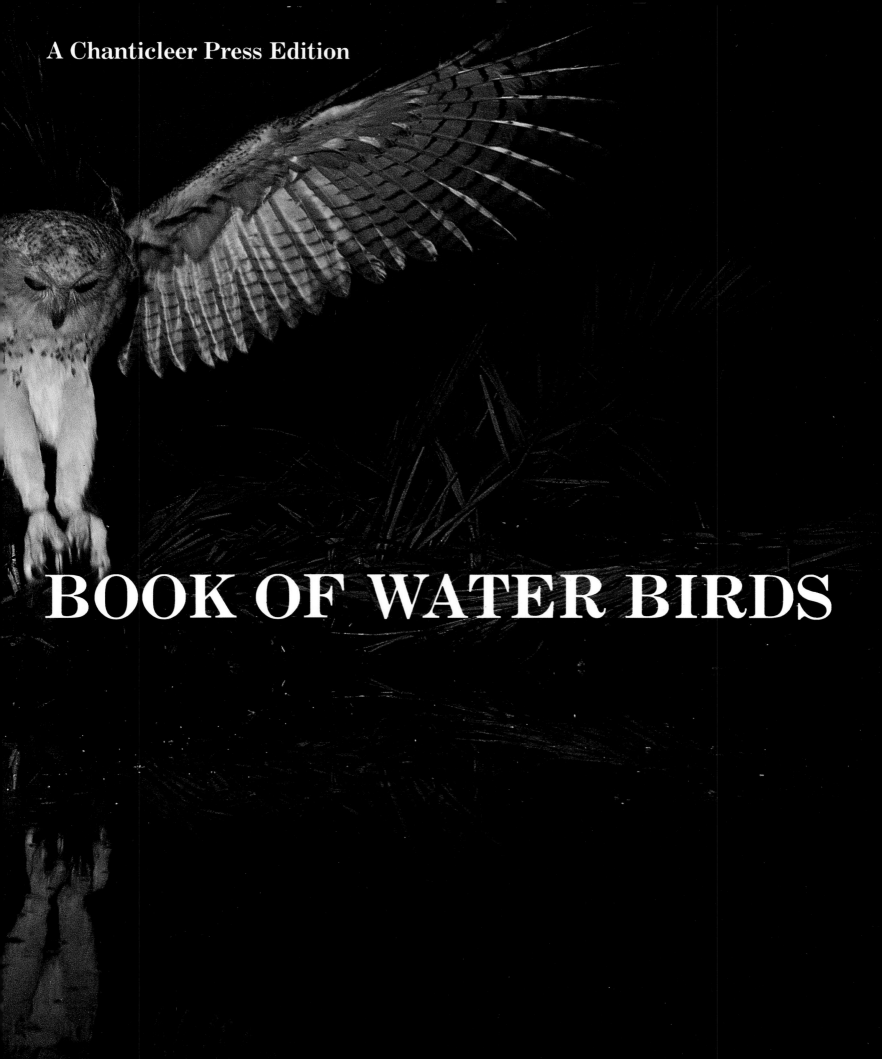

A Chanticleer Press Edition

BOOK OF WATER BIRDS

HARRY N. ABRAMS, INC., PUBLISHERS, NEW YORK

Library of Congress Cataloging-in-Publication Data
Line, Les.
The Audubon Society book of water birds.
"A Chanticleer Press edition."
Includes index.
1. Water-birds.   I. Garrett, Kimball.   II. National
Audubon Society.
III. Title.
QL673.L66   1987   598.29′24   87-1434
ISBN 0-8109-1863-3

Times Mirror Books

Trademark "Audubon Society" used by publisher under license by the National Audubon Society, Inc.

Prepared and produced by Chanticleer Press, Inc.
Manufactured in Japan

Chanticleer Staff
Publisher: Paul Steiner
Editor-in-Chief: Gudrun Buettner
Executive Editor: Susan Costello
Managing Editor: Jane Opper
Senior Editor: Ann Whitman
Associate Editor: David Allen
Assistant Editor: Craig Pospisil
Production: Helga Lose, Gina Stead-Thomas
Art Director: Carol Nehring
Art Associate: Ayn Svoboda
Art Assistant: Cheryl Miller
Picture Library: Edward Douglas
Natural Science Consultant: John Farrand, Jr.

Design: Massimo Vignelli

Frontispieces: *Swooping down to the water after dark in the Okavango Delta of Botswana in southern Africa, a rare Pel's fishing owl* (Scotopelia peli) *prepares to seize a fish its keen eyes have detected in the dim light. As it approaches its target, the owl brings its sharp talons forward and draws its head back. Then, with its face and eyes out of harm's way, the owl hits the surface feetfirst and with an audible splash, as its talons quickly snap closed.*

First overleaf: *Its splashing plunge a successful one, the Pel's fishing owl lifts its heavy catch from the surface with powerful downward beats of its wings, and heads toward a perch in the trees near the water.*

Second overleaf: *Sometimes a fish is so heavy, the owl seems almost to drag it over the surface and nearby shore, struggling to lift its prey to safety.*

Contents

Foreword

Ages before the first birds appeared, before any form of life
had left the water to colonize the land, the continents were
empty places. Ocean breakers rolled ceaselessly against sterile
shores of rock and sand, streams of rainwater cascaded down
the bare slopes of mountains, the still surfaces of lakes
reflected those ancient hills, and broad rivers flowed slowly
across a stark landscape and back into the sea.

As life evolved, invaded the land, and became ever more
complex, these basic water environments grew more
diversified as well. Variations in ocean temperature and
currents created a wide range of saltwater habitats, from
places where the water supported vast numbers of marine
creatures to seas that were almost without life. Still waters
now existed not only as lakes, but as densely forested swamps,
quiet ponds in woodlands and prairies, and extensive marshes
of grass, rushes, and reeds. Broad mudflats, rich with tiny
animals and plants, appeared wherever coastal lagoons were
protected from the pounding surf, and tidal marshes fringed
sheltered coves and bays. Rivers and streams now flowed
through environments of many kinds, and were as varied as
their surroundings. These new watery habitats contained life
that could serve as food for birds.

Experts still don't agree on exactly how it happened, but the
first birds, which evolved about 140 million years ago, were
feathered, flying creatures whose reptilian ancestors had
sprinted about on their hind legs. By the time these earliest
birds appeared, an elaborate aquatic banquet was waiting for
them. Although the first birds glided or flew among the
primitive trees of an ancient forest, freshwater and marine
environments offered a far more diverse array of habitats,
each with its own special food sources.

One of the most famous of fossils is *Archaeopteryx*, the
forerunner of all birds, an exquisitely preserved creature,
complete with feathers, that was found in 1861 in the Altmühl
region of Bavaria. It is not well known, however, that the first

really extensive deposits of fossil birds were found in beds of chalk in the Smoky Hills of western Kansas. All these Kansas fossils are the remains of water birds. They were inhabitants of a shallow sea that covered much of the interior of the United States about eighty million years ago. These Kansas seabirds included one called *Hesperornis*, or "western bird," that even at that early date had evolved flightlessness. A foot-propelled diver like a modern loon, it had wings that were so small they were not visible on the outside of the body; it also had sharp teeth, for seizing the fish that swam in those shallow seas of long ago.

Since the disappearance of this inland sea there has been ample time for a remarkable variety of water birds to evolve. While we do not have clear images of the vanished water birds of the past, the pages of this book contain striking views of the variety and beauty of the water birds of our own geological age. This wide-ranging portfolio includes the penguins, birds that have "reinvented" the flightlessness of *Hesperornis* to become the most accomplished of modern diving birds, as well as the shorebirds, each species with a bill that is a finely tuned instrument for capturing a special food or for catching prey in a unique way. Others among these birds of the water are the fish-catching eagles, hawks, and owls, birds of ancient lineage that are very likely the newest group of birds to adopt an aquatic way of life. Modern water birds must certainly be as rich an assortment as any geological period could boast.

With knowledgeable text by my friends Kimball Garrett and Kenn Kaufman, an abundance of superb photographs by seventy-nine celebrated photographers, all vividly described by Les Line, this book provides an unequalled introduction to the world's water birds. I hope it will make you want to see these wonderful birds for yourself.

John Farrand, Jr.

Preface

One of those picture-postcard sunsets hung over the darkening shores of Maine's Grand Lake as we tied our canoe to the camp dock. Ten miles long, Grand Lake is often thrashed by storms; but on this August evening, when the slightest breeze would have meant relief from the sweltering heat, not a ripple stirred the surface. Starting up the trail, I turned to admire the candy-striped sky just as the first peal of loon laughter rolled across the water.

Remember those demonstration records during the early days of stereophonic sound? One favorite trick was to have a steam locomotive, racing car, or jet plane approach from the distance through the left speaker, roar across your living room, then fade away through the right speaker. I was reminded of this as the loon, laughing all the way, flew from left to right across Grand Lake and disappeared behind a conifer-clad peninsula, its cry fading with the daylight.

It was not the first time I had heard the voice of the loon, but the circumstances had never been more dramatic. My thought at the moment was that no sound is more familiar to the North Country visitor; and that the wilderness would never again be whole should this voice be stilled. Back at camp, I thumbed through a well-read copy of Sigurd F. Olson's autobiography, *Open Horizons*, in search of one particular passage. Recalling his youthful guiding days in the Quetico-Superior canoe country of northern Minnesota, he wrote: "Each night we sat there looking down the waterway, listening to the loons filling the darkening narrows with wild reverberating music, but it was when they stopped that the quiet descended, an all-pervading stillness that absorbed all the sounds that had ever been. No one spoke. We sat there so removed from the rest of the world and with such a sense of complete remoteness that any sound would have been a sacrilege."

Many words have been used to describe the voice of the loon—words such as haunting, unearthly, eerie, mournful, piercing, maniacal, spine-tingling. Superstitious sailors once believed a wailing loon portended a tempest. Wrote John James Audubon, "In the course of a voyage from Charleston to the Florida Keys, in May 1832, I several times saw and heard loons . . . but not withstanding all the dire forebodings of the crew, who believed that a hurricane was at hand, our passage was exceedingly pleasant."

This tremolo call of the loon may either be given alone or performed antiphonally by a pair—that is, the call of the male will be quickly answered by the female, whose voice is pitched higher than her mate's. This sound, the familiar "maniacal" loon laughter, is thought to strengthen the pair bond, serve as a warning of danger, and coordinate behavior between the two birds if their territory is disturbed.

Of the five species of loons in the world, the one we know best is the common loon—the great northern diver of Europe. It breeds from Alaska, Greenland, and Iceland south to the northern United States; birds from Greenland and Iceland winter in Europe, from Great Britain to the Mediterranean Sea. But the voice of the loon is no longer heard in many of the bird's former haunts, particularly in New England. Loss of habitat to vacation home developments and disturbances by boaters have destroyed the privacy the loon demands for its presence, and the silence at night on these lakes is painful.

I talk of the loon at length because it is among the most remarkable water birds in the world, and my very favorite among many favorites. I am delighted that Paul Steiner and the editors at Chanticleer Press have chosen to celebrate this avian group with the eighth in a series of spectacular Audubon Society books. May it open new eyes to the wonderful birdlife that inhabits our lakes, streams, and marshes, our rocky seacoasts, oceanic islands, and estuaries, and help renew the determination of conservationists everywhere to preserve these fragile, threatened habitats.

Les Line

Below. *A black-crowned night-heron* (Nycticorax nycticorax) *lurks in the reeds of Las Marismas, a huge marsh in the Coto Doñana, the great European wildlife sanctuary on the coast of Spain. The black-crowned night-heron is considered the most numerous and cosmopolitan of all herons. In the New World, for instance, it breeds from the Canadian prairies to Tierra del Fuego and the Falkland Islands, nesting from sea level to a lake 15,800 feet high in the Chilean Andes. To avoid competition with other herons, it feeds from dusk to dawn on a remarkably diverse menu, including eels, spiders, small mammals, and nestlings of other birds.* (Guenter Ziesler)

Dancing Cranes and Other Waders

Into a sea of grass and shallow black water, twisting courses of slow-moving water slide out of a dark cypress swamp in southern Florida. This richly productive area is an ever-shifting meeting place of land and water; it isn't quite land and isn't quite lake, and it supports a teeming abundance of wildlife.

In the shade of a cypress tree at the edge of the sawgrass sea, long legs slice through the shallow water's surface, taking several hesitant, high-gaited steps, first in this direction, then that. The bird flexes its long neck downward as its five-inch-long bill pierces the water and the soft mud below. Seemingly random probes in the mud are followed by more steps, more probes. All at once the sensitive bill strikes the hard shell of a snail, and in a quick motion the mollusk is lifted out of the mud and above the water.

Our stalker is a limpkin (*Aramus guarauna*), a wading bird that lives in the more tropical parts of the New World from Florida into South America. A relative of the cranes as well as the rails and coots, the limpkin is distinct enough to be placed in its own family, the Aramidae. The limpkins are one of many families of long-legged wading birds that find their food primarily in shallow water. This limpkin has maneuvered the captured snail into the correct position in its bill—a supremely adapted snailing utensil.

The slight rightward bend to the tip of the upper mandible is perhaps an aid in the process of extracting snail meat from the shell. A small gap midway along the bill increases the bird's efficiency in holding rounded snail shells. With its prey in its bill, our limpkin takes several steps, then flies a short distance to an old cypress log, which will now serve as an anvil. The limpkin administers a few rapid blows, then extracts the snail with a probe and tug of the bill tip.

The limpkin's victim is an apple snail of the genus *Pomacea*. Studies have shown that this snail, abundant throughout

Florida's swamps and marshes, is an important component of the limpkin's diet. Having consumed its prey, the limpkin continues its slow and methodical search for snails in the shallow water.

In the marsh beyond, and along the winding courses of small, shallow rivers, hundreds of birds wade, like the limpkin, in pursuit of food. These shallow-water predators include herons, wood storks, ibises, spoonbills—a dozen species of long-legged waders that make their living in south Florida's interface of water and land.

In the heart of South America, the scene from the edge of Florida's everglades is played out on a vastly larger scale; on the Pantanal of southwestern Brazil and in nearby Paraguay, the Paraguay River and its tributaries seasonally flood the huge swampy area known as the Gran Chaco. Myriad wading birds, including snowy and great egrets (*Egretta thula* and *Casmerodius albus*), plumbeous and buff-necked ibises (*Harpiprion caerulescens* and *Theristicus caudatus*), roseate spoonbills (*Ajaia ajaja*), and huge jabiru storks (*Jabiru mycteria*) feed in these shallow waters; their variety provides an instant and memorable lesson in the diversity of design of long-legged waders. Half a world away, on the wet grasses that rim the shores of Kenya's Lake Nakuru, improbably adorned saddle-billed storks (*Ephippiorhynchus senegalensis*) walk in stately companionship with a variety of other waders. In the shallows of the lake itself, a fluid pink and white mass resolves itself into a hundred thousand greater and lesser flamingos (*Phoenicopterus ruber* and *Phoeniconaias minor*), whose long legs and necks seem at once impossibly long and impressively graceful.

Of more than 9,000 species of birds in today's world, the great majority live exclusively in terrestrial habitats. To be sure, some of these terrestrial species are as long-legged as the wading birds discussed here. Most of these inhabit grasslands. But unlike the long-legged waders of lakes and marshes, many of these birds do not fly well or often, and some never fly at all. Their long legs enable them to run and stalk in open plains environments. The secretary bird (*Sagittarius serpentarius*), a reptile-eater of East African grasslands, is thought to be allied with the hawks and eagles. The seriamas (family Cariamidae) of South America are distant, terrestrial relatives of the cranes. The various ratite birds, including the ostrich, rheas, cassowaries, and emus, have lost the ability to fly; they rely for safety and survival on their long, strong legs.

About 135 species belong to the five major families of long-legged wading birds: the herons (family Ardeidae), the storks (Ciconiidae), the ibises and spoonbills (Threskiornithidae), the flamingos (Phoenicopteridae), and the cranes (Gruidae). Placed in their own families, besides the limpkin we met above, are Africa's odd waders, the shoebill, or whale-headed stork (*Balaeniceps rex*) and the hammerkop (*Scopus umbretta*). While these birds share a superficially similar body plan, they have diverged in an array of ecological directions. From one of the world's most adaptable bird species, the cattle egret (*Bubulcus ibis*), to the highly specialized flamingos, limpkin, and shoebill, the long-legged waders engage in a rich variety of life-styles. Some, including many cranes, have evolved to forage in terrestrial situations, but even these birds remain linked to marshes in the nesting season.

Nature has constructed the legs of birds and humans—the only mammals that walk exclusively on their hind limbs—in slightly different ways. Compare the long, graceful leg of a great blue heron (*Ardea herodias*) to your own. Our knee joint gives a prominent forward bend to the leg, roughly at its mid-point, where the femur joins the tibia and fibula. The ankle joint, which attaches the foot to the leg, allows considerable movement and rotation. In a heron, however, the femur and knee joint are well inside the body, and the prominent, kneelike bend halfway down the leg is actually the bird's ankle! Thus the joint in the middle of a heron's leg bends in just the opposite way that our knee joint bends. The lower half of a bird's leg (called the tarsometatarsus) represents a number of fused heel and foot bones. The "foot" of a heron is really nothing more than its toes, and it is upon these four toes that herons walk.

The legs of all birds are built along this plan, with variations arising, in part, from the lengths of the different elements and the number and position of the toes. Ostriches possess only two toes; all other birds have three or four. The long-legged waders in this chapter all have three forward-directed toes and a fourth toe pointing backward; in the flamingos, this hind toe is greatly reduced or absent, and the front toes are connected by webbing.

The long legs of herons, storks, and other waders are complemented by long necks. This elongation of the neck is due in part to the extra length of individual vertebrae and in part to a larger number of these vertebrae. (In contrast, all mammals—even the long-necked giraffe—have only seven neck vertebrae.) The long necks of flamingos, cranes, and other waders are impressively flexible. The herons use their necks to make snakelike, forward thrusts for food. Herons fold their long necks neatly over the upper back in flight; other long-legged waders extend the neck forward in flight. And most waders have long bills that act in concert with the long neck to reach elusive prey.

Nearly half of the long-legged waders belong to the heron family, which includes some sixty species of herons, egrets, and bitterns. The members of this family share a generally similar body plan, including long necks that are folded in flight, long legs with a well-developed hind toe, and daggerlike bills. Variations on these themes include bills that range from the exceptionally long and thin, in the agami heron (*Agamia agami*), to shovel-like in the boat-billed heron (*Cochlearius cochlearius*). A heron's neck may be long and thin, as in the tricolored heron (*Egretta tricolor*), or relatively short, as in the night-herons (*Nycticorax*). In the overall design of their body features, however, members of the family are always easily recognizable as herons.

But there is more than one way to catch a fish—or a frog, a crab, or any of the other varied morsels that herons consume. And herons possess a remarkable repertoire of feeding techniques with which to catch these items. Perhaps most familiar is the slow, measured stalking in the shallows, where the time elapsed between steps might be measured in ten-second intervals, and the forward progress of the bill toward the haunts of the quarry evokes the anthropomorphic notion of "patience." Once the prey is sighted, it is captured with a rapid thrust of the bill. Among herons that employ this technique are the great egret, the large herons of the genus *Ardea*, the bitterns, and the small green-backed heron (*Butorides striatus*). Certain herons are more animated, and the reddish egret (*Egretta rufescens*) of tidal flats and brackish estuaries of the American tropics and subtropics carries animated feeding to a frenzied extreme. Running, flapping, and springing through the shallows, reddish egrets pursue fish, many of which are no doubt stirred up by the bird's movements.

Herons not only stalk their prey, but occasionally actively lure or disturb it. Cattle egrets, the most successful and rapidly increasing of the herons, follow large herds of game and cattle —and even farm tractors—to find and capture large insects. Snowy egrets frequently stand in shallow water, rapidly vibrating their bills at the water's surface—behavior that attracts fish much as we might by rippling the surface of a pond with our fingertips. The black heron (*Egretta ardesiaca*) of Africa often feeds by bringing its spread wings forward over its head to form a canopy, perhaps attracting prey to the shaded area below it. And some herons, in particular the widespread green-backed heron, are even known to attract prey with a lure—a feather or an insect larva dropped onto the water's surface!

Among the more specialized herons are the marsh-dwelling bitterns, cryptically colored and well known for their camouflaged "freeze" postures, and the night-herons, active primarily, as their name suggests, in darkness. Perhaps most unusual is the boat-billed heron of the New World tropics; this relative of the night-herons has a remarkably wide bill that probably increases feeding efficiency at night.

Herons nest in stick structures that may be on the ground, on bushes and mangroves, or even in tall trees. Courtship displays often involve elaborate plumes of "aigrettes"; these beautiful feathers were the height of human fashion for a time, and egret and heron rookeries were ravaged for the millinery trade—a slaughter that led to the founding of the first Audubon Societies in the late 1880s.

In their long-legged, long-necked structure, the seventeen species of storks somewhat resemble herons. But storks differ in a number of respects, including their heavier bodies and bills and their habit of flying with the neck extended. Many storks also have unfeathered areas on the head and neck. Most feed by slowly wading in shallow water, seizing a fish, amphibian, or crustacean with a sudden thrust of the bill. A few species, such as the white stork (*Ciconia ciconia*), famed for nesting on European rooftops and chimneys, frequently feed in fields well away from standing water, and their diets may include snakes, rodents, and insects such as locusts.

Some storks, including the huge and rather ungainly marabou (*Leptoptilos crumeniferus*) of Africa, augment their diet of aquatic and upland animals with carrion—the remains of dead animals. Marabou storks are characteristic attendants at animal kills on the plains of East Africa, waiting for the large predators to eat their fill. Like the vultures with which they share the carrion, marabous have strong bills, bare heads and necks, and ruffs at the base of their necks; they, too, soar on long, broad wings. The vultures associating with storks in Africa and elsewhere in the Old World are closely related to the hawks and eagles. But an entirely different group of vultures occurs in the Americas, and many ornithologists now believe that storks and New World vultures (including the rare condors and the familiar turkey and black vultures—*Cathartes aura* and *Coragyps atratus*) may be each other's closest relatives. They share a suite of adaptations for feeding on animal carcasses, and also have some unusual kinds of behavior in common.

Two large storks—the African marabou and the jabiru of the New World tropics—have exceptionally massive bills. These species and other storks often noisily clack their bills when displaying, generating an impressive mechanical clatter that augments a very limited repertoire of vocal sounds. The members of one group of storks, which includes the familiar wood stork (*Mycteria americana*) of the Americas, use their downcurved bills in a shallow-water feeding technique that relies largely on a sense of touch; the birds sweep the open mandibles through the water and along the bottom sediments, closing them when prey is contacted.

Like the limpkin, the two open-billed storks (*Anastomus*) of Asia and Africa have a gap between the upper and lower mandibles, midway along the bill. In these two storks the gap is very easy to see; its function in the extraction of mollusks from their shells is probably to provide the best angle of attack, rather than to serve as a "nutcracker" for gripping and splitting the shell.

Next to the herons, the largest group of long-legged waders contains the ibises and spoonbills. While anatomy and behavior suggest that these two groups of birds are closely related, their bills and feeding behavior have diverged markedly. All ibises have distinctively downcurved bills, with which they probe in shallows, mud, and upland soils. In the warmer parts of North America, the familiar ibises are the white, glossy, and white-faced (*Eudocimus albus, Plegadis falcinellus*, and

P. chihi); all are true wading birds, faithful to wetlands, shallows, and flooded areas. But some of the world's twenty-five or so ibises are upland birds, with little or no affinity to wetlands. The noisy and conspicuous hadada (*Hagedashia hagedash*) of sub-Saharan Africa is as likely to announce its presence on open savannahs, lawns, and in woodland clearings as it is in wetlands. The hermit ibis, or waldrapp (*Geronticus eremita*), of North Africa and the Middle East, is largely a bird of rocky cliffs in semidesert regions; it builds large stick nests in rocky crevices, but leaves its cliffside fastnesses in winter to forage in lowlands. Threatened by the pressures of human development on its specialized habitats, its population has declined to very low levels throughout its range.

Some ibises are clad in varying hues of dark brown, gray, and olive, and often show an iridescent sheen of green or purple; this iridescence (seen also in many ducks and some cormorants, rails, and other birds) is the result of the way the feathers refract light, rather than pigments. Many other ibises, such as the famous sacred ibis (*Threskiornis aethiopicus*) are largely white, or strikingly marked in black and white. The bright plumage of the aptly named scarlet ibis (*Eudocimus ruber*) of northern South America is unique in this group; closely related to the white ibis, which is widespread in the Americas, it has brilliant red plumage, due to pigments derived principally from its food.

The world's six spoonbills are in a sense ibises modified by evolution toward a very specialized bill structure and feeding technique. The flattened bill expands to a round, spoonlike tip, which the bird sweeps from side to side through shallow water and mud, closing it when prey is encountered. All the spoonbills are similar in general structure and habits. The five Old World species are mostly white in plumage, but the roseate spoonbill—the only one found in the New World—is suffused with pink, crimson, and orange.

Among the long-legged wading birds, one species stands out as an enigma as surely as it stands out against the backdrop of the tropical swamps in the upper reaches of the Nile. This is the shoebill, or whale-headed stork. Not a true stork, but perhaps an offshoot of that group, the shoebill is a huge, long-legged bird whose massive, swollen bill has a strong nail hooking over its tip. The bird's habit of flying with its neck retracted gives it an outwardly pelican-like appearance, and indeed some taxonomists have hypothesized that the shoebill is more closely related to the pelicans and their allies than to the storks.

Whatever its antecedents, the shoebill is an impressive and unusual bird. Its strong, deep bill is adapted for capturing fish —lungfish in particular—from water choked with submerged vegetation. Shoebills hunt by stalking slowly or standing motionless on floating vegetation in the vast but ever-shrinking swamps of its limited African range.

The shoebill is but one example of a bird that has confounded taxonomists by exhibiting an unusual mix of anatomical features. A more familiar group of long-legged waders, the flamingos, has likewise stymied ornithologists. Although flamingos are traditionally treated as relatives of the storks or herons, some experts believe that, because of certain characteristics, these large birds are related to the family of ducks, geese, and swans; and still other scientists link flamingos to the stilts and avocets. While the exact relationship of the flamingos to other birds remains an area of active debate, their mosaic of features teaches us that the products of evolution cannot always be neatly categorized; much remains to be learned from research into paleontology, anatomy, behavior, and biochemistry.

If family relationships were determined by feeding methods, flamingos might be likened to the baleen whales—for both are superbly adapted to filtering minute organisms from richly productive waters. Not sheets of baleen, but fine, hairlike lamellae fringe the interior of a flamingo's large, hooked bill; these lamellae catch the tiny food items taken in with the water or soft bottom mud, and the food is pulled into the digestive tract with rapid movements of the large, fleshy tongue. This very specialized feeding technique has allowed flamingos to flourish in salt lakes and alkali wetlands that are inhospitable to many other kinds of birds. Today, the world's five species of flamingos have become common—indeed often spectacularly abundant—in certain shallow lakes and estuaries of Africa and locally in the Andes, the tropical American coasts, and southernmost Eurasia. The fossil record shows that flamingos were once considerably more widespread, having inhabited much of Europe and North America.

The long, slender legs of a flamingo allow it to forage in the extensive shallows of lakes and estuaries; the webbed feet and ability to swim readily make flamingos unique among the long-legged waders. The flamingo's extraordinarily long neck is the mechanism that brings the bird's remarkable feeding apparatus down into shallow water and bottom sediments. In flight, the neck and legs are extended; but any comparison of this bird to a stretch-model goose cannot do justice to the flamingo's singular suite of adaptations.

Flamingos nest in large colonies; some colonies in Africa have been known to exceed a million pairs. Unlike most other waders, which nest in trees, shrubs, or other elevated situations, flamingos nest directly on the ground. They choose a mudflat, alkaline lake bed, salt pan, or gravel bed, and lay a single egg in a depression in the top of a small mound of mud. The newborn chick has a straight bill; the full feeding apparatus does not develop until the young bird is nearly three months old, and until that time it must continue to feed on a milky substance secreted by the parents.

The fifteen species of cranes are perhaps the most generalized of the long-legged wading birds, lacking any obvious modifications of the bill for special foraging techniques. The diet of cranes is correspondingly varied; on upland fields, these birds take different kinds of insects and vertebrate prey as well as plant items, and in shallow water they feed on crustaceans, fish, and other animals.

A majority of the world's cranes occur north of the equator, and the northernmost species migrate southward in the colder seasons. Australia has a nonmigratory crane, the brolga (*Grus rubicunda*); the similarly sedentary wattled crane (*Bugeranus carunculatus*) and blue crane (*Anthropoides paradisea*), along with the two species of crowned cranes (*Balearica*), reside in sub-Saharan Africa. Although storklike at first glance, the cranes are entirely unrelated to the storks, herons, and ibises. Instead, the cranes belong to a large hodgepodge of families, the order Gruiformes, which includes the rails and coots, the limpkin, and several small families of marsh-dwellers, grassland birds, and even forest species. Most of the features that distinguish cranes from the other groups of long-legged waders are anatomical; cranes also differ, however, in that their young mature more fully within the egg, and when they hatch, they are covered in rich down and are soon able to run around. Cranes also have loud, sonorous calls, given frequently to keep members of a pair or flock in contact.

The cranes have another feature that sets them apart: they are among the bird world's finest dancers. Bounding, jumping, and flapping variations on a terpsichorean theme characterize the courtship rituals of nearly all species. Such dances may be performed on the wintering grounds of migratory species, and they frequently are given in social contexts other than courtship; often many or all members of a large wintering congregation of cranes may unexpectedly launch into a bouncing ballet.

Changes over time in the size of the world's crane populations have provided ecologists with a twofold lesson. The diminution of crane populations has stood as testimony to man's sadly destructive impact on the living creatures of the planet. But— more optimistically—the recovery of certain species from near extinction attests to man's ability to reverse these population declines. Three spectacular white species breeding in the Far North—the Japanese crane (*Grus japonensis*), the Siberian white crane (*Grus leucogeranus*), and North America's whooping crane (*Grus americana*)—have suffered drastic population declines over the last century. The sandhill crane (*Grus canadensis*) of North America provides the spectacle of flocks numbering in the thousands in some parts of its winter and migratory range, but even this species has dwindled precariously in Cuba and on the Gulf Coast of the United States.

Diligent work by scientists and conservationists has shown that careful management and habitat protection, combined in some cases with captive breeding, can give hope to the long-term survival of these and other species. The cranes, which over the centuries have engendered wonder and reverence through their beauty, dancing, and migrations, are symbolic of what is right and what is wrong in the fragile relationship between humans and the environment.

Opposite. *A saddle-billed stork (Ephippiorhynchus senegalensis) hunts frogs, lizards, and small mammals in tall grass near the edge of a swamp in Kenya's Amboseli Reserve. Standing more than four feet tall, the saddle-bill is one of the largest storks, and certainly the most colorful, with its tremendous, sharply pointed bill topped by the saddlelike shield that gives the bird its name. The saddle-billed stork is found from Ethiopia to Senegal to South Africa, nesting in solitary pairs in swamps and on lakeshores. Although closely related to the loquacious herons, storks lack a voice box and thus are mute. They make up for this vocal shortcoming by loudly clattering their bills.* (Dale and Marian Zimmerman)

First overleaf. *As unattractive as the saddle-billed stork is handsome, the marabou stork (Leptoptilus crumeniferus) has a huge, wedge-shaped bill designed for ripping into carrion. The marabou soars over Africa like a vulture and has a nearly naked head for probing animal carcasses. This large bird dominates the inevitable crowd of carrion-feeders at the remains of a lion kill, for it must eat two pounds of meat a day. Marabous nest at the end of the rainy season, because there is more carrion during the dry months, and aquatic life is concentrated in shrinking ponds. They are nicknamed "adjutants," for their style of marching about is reminiscent of the starchy, solemn manner of army officers.* (Dale and Marian Zimmerman)

Second overleaf. *With its long bill, a tricolored heron (Egretta tricolor) juggles a minnow that it has nabbed from a Florida Everglades pond. A bird of salt marshes, bayous, mudflats, and lagoons from Long Island to the Amazon delta on the Atlantic Coast, and from southern California to Peru on the Pacific shore, the tricolored heron dashes about nervously in search of small fish, crayfish, and shrimp. It nests in dense colonies with other herons, rarely building its solid platform more than ten feet from the ground.* (Larry West)

Above. *The crow-sized green-backed heron* (Butorides striatus) *occurs worldwide, in nearly every type of wetland habitat—from woodland ponds in the north, where it is the only resident heron, to coastal mangrove swamps in tropical latitudes. Stalking minnows, crayfish, and aquatic and terrestrial insects, the green-backed heron stretches its neck and bill forward, takes a deliberate step or two, aims, and stabs. When flushed from hiding, it utters a rasping, exasperated squawk and flies only a short distance.* (C. Allan Morgan)

Left. *The limpkin* (Aramus guarauna) *"limps" through freshwater swamps from Georgia to Argentina, using its long, downcurved bill to wrest snails from their shells. By night, it rends the darkness with its spooky, human-sounding wail. The size of a goose, the limpkin is the only species in its family; scientists consider it an evolutionary link between cranes and rails. Its long toes and sharp claws are designed for striding over muck and emergent vegetation; it swims easily in deeper water, but it takes to the air reluctantly, soon fluttering back into the marsh.* (Ben Goldstein/Root Resources)

Overleaf. *Once recognized as a separate species, the lava heron of the Galapagos Islands is now considered a subspecies of the green-backed heron. Its slate-gray color blends with the lava rocks that it shares with a crimson marine crab called the Sally lightfoot* (Grapsus grapsus). *Prawns are a staple of this bird's diet, but the lava heron also hunts lizards in the cactus forests and cockroaches in the settlement of Academy Bay.* (François Gohier)

31

Right. *Droplets of water fly in all directions as an adult great blue heron* (Ardea herodias) *grapples with a fish. It is the most widespread member of the heron family in North America. Because of its large size, the great blue can capture the greatest variety of prey, from tiny minnows to fish too big for most other herons to handle, and so it can forage almost anywhere.* (Tim Fitzharris)

Top two rows. *Darting and dancing in the surf on a Texas beach, a dark adult little blue heron (Egretta caerulea) pursues small fish as they struggle against the turbulent currents of the waves. Unlike the dark adults, which generally hunt alone, young little blue herons tend to fish in groups, and are almost pure white. Their white color is thought to be a signal to other birds, announcing that a good fishing place has been found. As the birds mature and acquire dark feathers, their feeding habits change from social to solitary.* (Steven C. Wilson/Entheos)

Above, bottom row right. *Here a young great blue heron feeds in the same surf as the little blue heron, but it does so in a slower and more dignified manner, stalking majestically through the shallows, watching for a fish or crab to show itself. It is equally at home in marshes, shallow rivers, and ponds.* (Steven C. Wilson/Entheos)

Above. *Called* Grus japonensis *by ornithologists, and* tancho *by the Hokkaido farmers who scatter corn for these stately birds during the winter, the Japanese cranes signal the coming of spring by engaging in spectacular courtship dances—leaping, flapping their wings, and arching their necks in graceful curves—all accompanied by loud bugling calls. Soon the three hundred birds that survive in Japan will depart for their more northerly breeding grounds. Another seven hundred Japanese cranes are still to be found on the Asian mainland, in China, Siberia, and Korea.* (François Gohier)

Opposite. *Declared a Special National Treasure by the government of Japan, the Japanese crane had dwindled from thousands to only thirty-three birds by 1952 because of habitat destruction. Now a marshland refuge and strict conservation laws provide adequate protection for these birds. They have always been a symbol of happiness and marital fidelity to the Japanese, and now they have become a symbol of what effective conservation measures can accomplish.* (François Gohier)

Opposite. *One million lesser flamingos* (Phoeniconaias minor) *filter 150 tons of blue-green algae a day from the alkaline soup of Kenya's Lake Nakuru. The most abundant flamingo in the world, this species numbers four million birds in East Africa, and another two million elsewhere on the continent. Both the flamingo's bill and its feeding method are unique in the world of birds. The bill is held upside down, with water and mud pumped by throat action through slits on the top bill and toothlike projections on the bird's oversized tongue, to strain out animal and plant life.* (Yann Arthus- Bertrand/Jacana)

Above. *A pair of Andean flamingos* (Phoenicoparrus andinus) *takes flight from a lake 12,000 feet high in the mountains of Chile. The flamingo nest—a cone of mud a foot in diameter—holds a single egg in a saucerlike hollow at the top. Male and female share incubation duties, sitting atop the mound with their long legs folded beneath them.* (François Gohier)

Above. *Like other Old World spoonbills, the African spoonbill* (Platalea alba) *is pale of plumage. To feed, spoonbills stride through shallow water, swinging their half-open bills back and forth, scooping up crustaceans, small fish, and aquatic insects.* (N.R. Christensen)

Opposite. *In contrast to its African relative, the roseate spoonbill* (Ajaia ajaja) *of North and South America is distinctly pink. This species was nearly exterminated from the southern United States by plume-hunters because of milliners' demands for its glorious pink feathers. Spoonbills raise three to five young, which feed by thrusting their bills deep into the throat of a parent.* (Tim Fitzharris)

Opposite. *Scouring the brushy edge of a freshwater pond at Brigantine National Wildlife Refuge on the New Jersey shore, a cattle egret* (Bubulcus ibis) *in breeding plumage has made an unusual catch—a female cecropia moth* (Platysamia cecropia) *with a copulating male still attached. This commonplace Old World egret crossed the Atlantic to South America a century ago, reached Florida around 1940, and has since spread rapidly across the United States; many biologists fear that it will compete for increasingly scarce nesting sites, and threaten native herons and egrets.* (Robert Villani)

Above. *The reddish egret* (Egretta rufescens), *a bird of saltwater lagoons from the Gulf Coast of the United States to Central America, has two color phases: some birds are totally white, others gray with a rusty head and neck. The proportion of white birds in a colony ranges from perhaps four percent on the Texas coast to nearly ninety percent in the Bahamas. Breeding adults have a shaggy "mane" that led to the species' extirpation from Florida by plume-hunters, but over the past half-century the reddish egret has returned in modest numbers. It forages with wings extended, creating pools of shadow that make it easier to spot fish.* (Steven C. Kaufman)

Top and opposite. *Symbol of the National Audubon Society, the great egret* (Casmerodius albus) *was the primary target of plume-hunters in southern swamps. The lacy plumes on its back—called "aigrettes" in the millinery trade—were worth their weight in gold: $32 an ounce in 1903. But to get one ounce of plumes, four egrets had to be slain. The extent of the slaughter is told by one statistic: In 1898, plumes of 1,538,000 "white herons" were shipped from Venezuela. And the shooting took a greater toll than just the adult birds killed by poachers, because chicks and eggs perished unattended.* (Steven C. Wilson/Entheos; Lynn M. Stone)

Above. *The snowy egret* (Egretta thula) *of North and South America was likewise exploited by poachers because of its curse of beauty: the fifty upswept plumes on its back and its long, lacy crown.* (Rita Summers/Amwest)

Overleaf. *Drowned cottonwood trees in California's Salton Sea house the platform nests of great egrets, snowy egrets, and great blue herons. Marine fish and invertebrates transplanted from the Gulf of California have thrived here, bringing pelicans, cormorants, herons, waterfowl, and vast numbers of migrant shorebirds.* (G.C. Kelley)

Below. *With a population exceeding two million, the lesser snow goose* (Chen caerulescens) *is probably the most abundant of all wild geese. It breeds in the Arctic from Wrangel Island in Siberia to Baffin Island in eastern Canada, and its colonies are huge—up to 100,000 pairs, with 3,000 nests crowded into a square mile of tundra. The female incubates the half-dozen eggs in a down-lined cup of moss and grass. Migrating through the middle of North America to the Gulf Coast and down the Pacific Flyway to California, lesser snow geese fly in wavy lines at altitudes as high as 20,000 feet, constantly yelping like terriers.* (John Cancalosi/Tom Stack and Associates)

Dabblers, Grazers, and Divers

What a simple task to describe a duck! Start with webbed feet and a duck bill; add strong wings, a long neck, a loud quack—and you have it. These are the salient features of a most familiar fowl, from barnyard to park pond, from Japanese screen painting to cartoon. Yet obviously, there is more to a duck than that. To do justice to the description of the waterfowl, to touch on the beauty and the mystery of the diverse members of this family, requires the talents of a poet, an artist, and a keen student of birds.

The ducks, geese, and swans that form the family Anatidae—a uniform group to the taxonomist—display a richness of diversity in both plumage and behavior that belies their close relationship. Many family members are cloaked in pure white, like most swans, or somber mottled browns, like many female dabbling ducks; but other ducks exhibit the most detailed and colorful patterning of any water birds, or indeed among any birds.

A close look at the plumage of a wood duck (*Aix sponsa*) reveals the beauty to be found among the waterfowl. Iridescent green and magenta on the crest give way to a striking black-and-white face pattern of subtly glossed, velvety feathers. The maroon chest is spangled with small white chevrons, while the fanlike feathers of the golden-brown flanks are finely and delicately etched with black vermiculations. The sheen on the wings and tail changes when light strikes it at different angles, varying from steel-blue to purple, from bronze to black. The wood duck and its perhaps even more gaily colored relative, the Asian mandarin duck (*Aix galericulata*), are striking in their beauty and, consequently, widely kept for their ornamental value. But beauty is more than feather-deep; it is an intangible attribute of even the plainest waterfowl.

A survey of the diverse members of the duck family easily demonstrates that a duck is, after all, not just a duck. The family of ducks, geese, and swans is divided into three subfamilies and ten tribes (groupings of related genera). Among these groups are upland grazers, mud-sifters, fish-catchers, and mollusk-eaters. While a few species hardly ever get wet, others are among the most accomplished divers. Variations in the bill are many, from the plant-cutting tool of some geese to the sievelike strainer of the shovelers and the slender, saw-toothed bill of the mergansers. Most ducks are strong and swift in flight, but two species of South American steamer-ducks cannot fly at all—and nearly every duck loses its powers of flight during a brief period of molt. The waterfowl include one of the heaviest of flying birds, the twenty-eight-pound trumpeter swan (*Cygnus buccinator*), as well as certain small teals and pygmy-geese, which weigh in at twelve ounces or less.

Waterfowl have become successful in nearly every aquatic habitat on the earth, apart from the pelagic realm of the oceans. Coastlines, tundra bogs, every kind of lake and pond, and even the swiftest torrents have their resident waterfowl. Migrant flocks of waterfowl have flown higher into the skies than any other kind of bird; a flock of bar-headed geese (*Anser indicus*) was once recorded traveling over the crest of the Himalayas. Wanderers have reached the most distant oceanic islands, and some islands have unique, isolated populations, such as the koloa of Hawaii, now considered a race of the mallard (*Anas platyrhynchos*); some of these races are distinct enough to be considered full species. Waterfowl, furthermore, are often very abundant where they occur, particularly in migration and on wintering grounds. Vast flocks spring into flight or wing past, high overhead—the traffic of the wilderness criss-crossing in the air. Their flight is strong and direct, and their flocks are often arranged to some subtle advantage in distinctive lines or V formations. While these flights are evocative of notions of freedom and wildness, waterfowl remain among our most familiar birds, and few park ponds, even in the hearts of our cities, are without them.

Among the factors that account for the abundance and success of most waterfowl species surely must be their strong powers of flight. Powerful wings take flocks of waterfowl from protected resting or nesting areas to productive feeding areas on a daily basis, and between breeding grounds and wintering grounds annually. This daily and seasonal exploitation of different habitats for different purposes characterizes most ducks, geese, and swans. Their strong, swift flight is powered by well-developed flight muscles attached to a large keel on the sternum, or breastbone.

The largest of the waterfowl are the swans, famed for their lovely, long-necked grace and their spectacularly large size. Moreover, the beauty and spectacle of a single swan may be multiplied a thousand times over or more, as the migratory species gather in flocks. The tundra swan (*Cygnus columbianus*) is the most abundant and widespread species over most of the northern hemisphere; its North American populations are concentrated into two major wintering areas, the Central Valley of California and the Chesapeake Bay region of Maryland, Virginia, and Delaware. In certain locations, as many as 25,000 birds flock together; just a little bit of ornithological arithmetic tells us this amounts to nearly 200 tons of swans! It is little wonder that their aesthetic impact is so profound.

There are three other northern species of swans: the whooper swan (*Cygnus cygnus*) of Eurasia, its close North American relative the trumpeter swan, and the mute swan (*Cygnus olor*) of the Old World. The mute swan has had a long association with man; its curve-necked grace now commonly adorns parts of the Atlantic Coast in the United States, where the species has been introduced. The trumpeter swan, once severely reduced in numbers, now totals several thousand birds, which occur in scattered refuges and large parks in northwestern North America.

Three other swans live in the southern hemisphere, and two of these depart from the pure-white plumage of our familiar northern swans. The black-necked swan (*Cygnus melanocoryphus*) and the odd Coscoroba swan (*Coscoroba coscoroba*) live in southern South America; the black-necked is white except for the marking suggested by its name. The Australian black swan (*Cygnus atratus*) usually appears entirely black, its white wing quills showing only in flight.

Swans feed primarily upon aquatic vegetation. Their large size and extraordinarily long necks allow them to feed efficiently on the bottom and margins of ponds, reaching material unavailable to other nondiving waterfowl. Swans have strong bills adapted for tearing free submerged grasses, stems, and tubers, although these birds are also capable of straining duckweed and other vegetation from the water's surface, in a manner reminiscent of many ducks.

Geese are familiar to us on several levels. The well-known goose of barnyard and fairy tale is usually a domesticated descendant of one of several northern species, such as Europe's famous greylag (*Anser anser*) or the circumpolar greater white-fronted goose (*Anser albifrons*). In a somewhat broader sense, the term "goose" is applied to some fourteen species of the northern hemisphere, all closely related to one another and placed in the same tribe as the swans. The familiar geese of North America, such as the Canada goose (*Branta canadensis*), belong in this group. Finally, in its broadest sense, the name goose is also used for a number of moderately large waterfowl of tropical or southern temperate regions; these geese, such as the South American kelp goose (*Chloephaga hybrida*), are not closely related to the northern species.

Nearly all of these geese have a strong, rather stout bill adapted for clipping and grazing vegetation. While many geese feed on submerged vegetation, most species are also quite at home on pasturelands and grain fields, where they graze in the style of deer or other mammals. One species, the nene (*Branta sandvicensis*) of the Hawaiian Islands, has taken the terrestrial route to an extreme, living its life on the volcanic slopes of the main island of Hawaii, far from water. The nene grazes on terrestrial plants, and the webbing of the feet, of no use on volcanic terrain, has been greatly reduced during a long period of isolation from the bird's mainland ancestor.

Northern geese are highly migratory, moving seasonally between breeding areas on tundra or the arctic coasts and wintering areas in temperate zones. In North America only the widespread Canada goose breeds south of Alaska and northern Canada, with some populations nesting south to marshes of the prairies and Great Basin. The best known of American geese, the Canada goose exhibits a fascinating geographical variation, especially in size. The largest subspecies, from the prairie regions, weigh more than three times as much as the smallest Arctic race. Like many other waterfowl, Canada geese gather from widely scattered breeding regions to just a handful of temperate wintertime refuges; on wintering grounds, a variety of large and small races may occur together.

Most ornithologists recognize a series of "flyways" along which migrant geese and ducks generally travel. With the change of seasons come the migrating geese, flying in formation along these fairly predictable routes, their appearance one of the more indelible reminders of the order of nature. With foresight and careful good sense we can ensure that these flyways will continue to provide an avenue of safe travel for tens of thousands of geese each fall and spring.

The snow goose (*Chen caerulescens*) occurs in two color phases, one mainly white and the other (known as the "blue" goose) a slaty gray-blue. Snow geese flock abundantly in much of North America, joined locally in parts of western North America by their diminutive white relative, Ross' goose (*Chen rossii*). Oddly, there are no white geese native to Eurasia— although individual snow geese have been known to turn up from time to time; instead, the basic goose is chiefly represented by the greylag and several relatives of the greater white-fronted goose. The grazing habits of some geese, notably the various forms of the brant (*Branta bernicla*), are directed toward marine habitats, where large populations winter on bays and feed primarily on eelgrass.

Several "geese" from the southern continents are not close relatives of the northern true geese, but rather isolated members of the tribe that includes the common shelduck (*Tadorna tadorna*) of Europe. The shelducks occur in much of the Old World and in many ways suggest a link between the geese and the ducks. The most widespread species, the common shelduck, is found mainly on estuaries and seacoasts, and around saline inland lakes; shelducks are far more omnivorous in their habits than the related southern geese (often called "sheldgeese").

Visitors to the African tropics commonly encounter the conspicuous Egyptian goose (*Alopochen aegyptiacus*) which, like the true geese, is a grazing vegetarian. Some other grazing geese live in the colder parts of South America. The

Andean goose (*Chloephaga melanoptera*) lives far up in the rugged mountains, near high, cold alpine lakes. The kelp goose feeds on seaweed along rocky shorelines. Males and females show the most extreme sexual differences in plumage of any waterfowl; the males are pure white, while the females are deep blackish-brown above and heavily barred below.

Because of their numbers and their wide distribution, the dabbling ducks of the genus *Anas* perhaps rank as the best known of the waterfowl. The familiar and widely domesticated mallard exhibits many recurrent traits of this group: a distinctive bright drake plumage that contrasts with the more cryptic feathering of the hen; massive seasonal migratory movements; and a feeding style that involves tipping up, or up-ending, in shallow water. Not burdened with the body and limb modifications necessary for diving (as are the diving ducks we will meet later on), the dabbling ducks can walk on land with relative ease, albeit with a certain lack of grace; they can also spring straight into flight from land or from the water's surface. Their realm, therefore, encompasses shore and water, from grain fields and mudflats to the margins and shallows of ponds, lakes, and estuaries. At rest or in migration, dabbling ducks are also at home on deeper water, and the odd flock of migrants resting on the ocean is not an unusual sight. Within their realm, the dabbling ducks are often spectacularly abundant—a testimony to the evolutionary success of their build and behavior.

The dabbling ducks have both benefited and suffered at the hands of people; management policies are often selectively directed toward the maintenance of duck habitats and populations, and such management can be very successful when applied toward both breeding and wintering areas. But the draining of nesting and wintering wetland habitats for development has had a harmful impact in many regions, and in some places the birds suffer from local overhunting.

The most familiar dabbling ducks—the mallards, pintails, teals, shovelers, and wigeons—are anatomically rather similar to one another, but still exhibit many variations in their feeding techniques. With their relatively stubby bills, for example, the three species of wigeons graze, goose-fashion, on terrestrial plants as well as submerged shallow-water plants. The northern shoveler (*Anas clypeata*) and its relatives in the southern hemisphere have a broad, spoonlike bill used as a sieve for straining small aquatic animals, as well as plants and seeds, from the shallow water. The combined action of a thick, fleshy tongue and fine lamellae on the borders of the expanded bill accomplish this feeding in a manner recalling the flamingos. In their feeding adaptations, the shovelers are not freakish offshoots, but rather the extreme of a gradation in bill size and lamellae development that can be traced from the garganey (*Anas querquedula*) and the blue-winged teal (*Anas discors*), to the cinnamon teal (*Anas cyanoptera*). The smallest dabbling duck is the green-winged teal (*Anas crecca*). It feeds on small seeds and other plant material on the muddy margins of lakes, ponds, and estuaries.

More distantly related to the *Anas* ducks are several species with diverse feeding adaptations. The torrent duck (*Merganetta armata*), at home in swift-flowing streams in the Andes of South America, is slender-bodied and narrow-billed, and feeds mainly on insect larvae; it may use its long, stiff tail as an aid in balancing and perching on slippery streamside rocks, much as certain cormorants use their tails. The blue duck (*Hymenolaimus malacorhynchus*) of New Zealand also lives in mountain streams, feeding on insect larvae and algae with its almost tubular bill.

It is generally true that male and female dabbling ducks show distinctly different plumages. In most dabblers, the colorful breeding plumage of the drake serves a vital function in courtship and pair formation. In nearly all species, the male passes through an accelerated molting period in late summer, when it briefly wears a mottled "eclipse" plumage resembling the plumage of the female. During this molt, all the flight feathers are dropped almost simultaneously, resulting in a short period of flightlessness. The showy breeding (or "nuptial") plumage is regained soon after flocks arrive on the wintering grounds, and pairs usually form late in the winter. It is the hen who makes the selection of a mate—a choice based in large part on the distinctive plumage and the courtship displays of the male. Thus the acquisition of the bright nuptial plumage by the males is a signal that starts off the pairing process—and timing is critical in the annual cycle of migratory waterfowl. In nonmigratory dabblers—such as the mottled duck (*Anas fulvigula*) of the Gulf Coast and many dabbling ducks of the Southern Hemisphere—the males are hardly different in appearance from the females.

Several tribes of waterfowl make their living by diving, exploiting deep-water habitats for both animal and vegetable food. Diving ducks propel themselves underwater by their strong, webbed feet. For diving efficiency, the legs are placed toward the rear of the body, and the wings are relatively smaller than the wings of waterfowl that do not dive. Most diving ducks are nonetheless strong fliers, and many are as highly migratory as the swans, geese, and dabbling ducks. Reduction of the wing is carried to an extreme, however, in the steamer-ducks (*Tachyeres*), four closely related marine ducks of southern South America. These birds are accomplished divers, but their powers of flight are reduced or nonexistent.

The group known as pochards includes several familiar Eurasian and North American species: the common pochard (*Aythya ferina*), the canvasback (*Aythya valisineria*), the redhead (*Aythya americana*), the ring-necked duck (*Aythya collaris*), the tufted duck (*Aythya fuligula*), and the greater and lesser scaups (*Aythya marila* and *Aythya affinis*). In some ways, the pochards seem to link the dabbling ducks with the more specialized divers. Pochards feed on plant and animal matter, and wintering rafts of many of the northern species can be impressively large. Unlike the dabblers, however, many of these diving species winter on salt water.

One group of diving ducks, the eiders, is limited to the cold coastal areas of the Far North. In these inhospitable waters, the four hardy eider species dive for mollusks and crustaceans. Two species, the common and king eiders (*Somateria mollissima* and *Somateria spectabilis*) occur in both northern oceans; the Steller's (*Polysticta stelleri*) and spectacled eiders (*Somateria fischeri*) are restricted to the waters off Siberia and Alaska. Nesting in these rigorous climates is not without its challenges; eiders—like many other waterfowl—have ameliorated these conditions by lining their nests with down feathers plucked from their own breasts. Long harvested by man, soft eiderdown has remarkable powers of insulation; consider how often you put on a covering of waterfowl feathers to keep warm! Male eiders are also notable for the plush, velvety feathering on the head, soft to the touch and stunning to look at.

Among the other sea ducks, the three species of scoters in the genus *Melanitta* use their strong bills and excellent diving powers to feed upon mollusks. The smaller-billed harlequin duck (*Histrionicus histrionicus*) also depends upon crustaceans in its winter haunts along rocky coastlines; during breeding season, it feeds mainly on insect larvae in the swift flowing streams where it nests. The oldsquaw (*Clangula hyemalis*), another crustacean feeder, may routinely dive to depths of 50 to 100 feet; like many sea ducks, oldsquaws nest on arctic tundra, consuming insects, small fish, and a variety of other items during the summer months.

Fishing among ducks is accomplished most successfully by the mergansers, whose long, saw-toothed bills enable them to capture and hold onto slippery prey. Two large species, the common merganser (*Mergus merganser*, called the "goosander" in English-speaking Europe) and the red-breasted merganser (*Mergus serrator*) are widespread across the Northern Hemisphere. The New World and Old World each has its own smaller species, the hooded merganser (*Lophodytes cucullatus*) and the smew (*Mergellus albellus*), respectively. Two other mergansers, one in Brazil and another in China, are quite rare; the seventh, once found only on the Auckland Islands south of New Zealand, is now extinct. Their slender bodies, strong legs, and webbed feet confer on the mergansers the ability to maneuver swiftly underwater in pursuit of their darting prey.

Barrow's goldeneye and the common goldeneye (*Bucephala islandica* and *Bucephala clangula*), together with their sprightly little cousin, the bufflehead (*Bucephala albeola*) are considered the closest relatives of the mergansers. The goldeneyes are often identified by the whistling of their wings as they fly in compact, fast-moving flocks. All three are expert divers, pursuing aquatic larvae, crustaceans, and small fishes with ease.

The stifftails form a tribe of diving ducks quite distinct in many ways from all other waterfowl. As seen in their most familiar representative, the ruddy duck (*Oxyura jamaicensis*), the stifftails are characterized by heavy bodies, small wings, legs placed well toward the rear of the body, and the peculiar long, stiff tail suggested by their name. Stifftails dive for a variety of animal and vegetable food items in marshy ponds and estuaries and on more open lakes.

The name "waterfowl" is no accident; the ducks, geese, and swans are creatures of the water, and access to wetlands or open-water feeding and resting sites is a critical component of the daily and seasonal routines of nearly all species. Simply put, a duck is at home on the water, or waddling on a nearby shore or prairie. But a surprising number of waterfowl are also at home in trees. Indeed, several of the groups mentioned above, including the goldeneyes and the mergansers, include species that nest in tree cavities.

There is one tribe of waterfowl whose members all habitually perch and nest in trees. These perching ducks include the Muscovy duck (*Cairina moschata*) of the New World tropics, a species that has been widely domesticated throughout the world. Muscovies inhabit forested rivers and swamps, nesting in tree hollows; related species occur in the Old World tropics. The wood duck of North America nests in tree cavities up to fifty feet or more above the forest floor. The young of these and other cavity-nesting ducks are able to jump safely to ground level well before they are capable of sustained flight.

The eight species of whistling-ducks form a distinctive group; despite their size and general ducklike appearance, they are probably allied most closely with the swans and geese. Many whistling-ducks perch readily in trees, as the alternate group name "tree-duck" suggests; certain species, such as the black-bellied whistling-duck (*Dendrocygna autumnalis*) of the American tropics, nest in tree cavities. Whistling-ducks occur in tropical and subtropical regions, feeding mainly on plant material. Long-necked and long-legged, they have a distinctive hunch-backed and broad-winged flight profile. Both perched and in flight, they utter the whistled calls for which they are named.

Variations in the world of waterfowl extend in many directions away from our standard notion of a duck. One last waterfowl group, represented by the unique magpie-goose (*Anseranas semipalmatus*) of Australia, has evolved such unducklike features as nearly unwebbed toes and proportionately very long legs. Magpie-geese are marshland waders and perch readily in trees. They perhaps link the waterfowl with the three screamers (Anhimidae), a small group of South American terrestrial and marshland birds that share a number of anatomical features with the waterfowl—yet outwardly, the screamers conform in no way to our concept of a goose or duck.

More than any other group of birds, the diverse yet familiar waterfowl have provided a strong basis for man's aesthetic and scientific appreciation of the avian kingdom. And with wise management of our planet's wetlands, their numbers and beauty will continue to sustain this appeal.

Opposite and first overleaf. *Groups of Canada geese* (Branta canadensis) *are a perfect addition to many a scene in wild America: a frosty October morning on the Firehole River in Yellowstone National Park, a frozen winter marsh at Blackwater National Wildlife Refuge in Maryland. The sight and sound of migrating Canada geese, with their perfect V-shaped formations and the musical honking that fills the spring and autumn skies, rarely fails to stir the watcher's spirit. But to many urban and suburban residents, the Canada goose has become a pest—a paddling, waddling "pigeon" that weighs up to twenty-six pounds. Freed from the pressures of hunting and predation that control wild populations, the urban geese thrived, and today hundreds of thousands of Canada geese live in cities from Boston to Seattle. Greenswards and golf courses are deep in droppings; goose-polluted ponds are closed to swimmers; and these feathered honkers are a traffic hazard along parkways. Efforts to control burgeoning urban goose populations have met with little success.* (Tom and Pat Leeson; Jack Dermid)

Second and third overleaves. *Imported from Eurasia to grace the estates of the wealthy, the magnificent mute swan* (Cygnus olor) *has also become something of a problem bird in North America. Michigan's 1,000 resident mute swans are the descendants of a pair of birds liberated in 1919; another 2,000 mute swans inhabit coastal wetlands from Massachusetts to Maryland. One of the heaviest flying birds, they easily rout any intruder with flailing wings and vicious bites. Biologists worry that all native waterfowl will be driven from mute swan nesting territories, which can cover ten acres.* (Tim Zurowski; Guenter Ziesler)

Opposite. *A century ago, when the feathers of wild birds were popular embellishments of women's fashions, thousands of black-necked swans (Cygnus melanocoryphus) were killed for their striking plumage. The black-necked swan is found in the southern third of South America and in the Falkland Islands. This small swan is adapted for efficient swimming, with legs far back on its body; thus it is as clumsy as a loon when it comes ashore, pushing itself forward on its breast.* (Lynn Rogers)

Above. *A white-tipped crimson bill accents the funereal plumage of the black swan (Cygnus atratus). When the swan is afloat, its snow-white wing feathers are hidden; in flight, they flash brilliantly. A long, snakelike neck also distinguishes this Australian native.* (Tim Fitzharris)

Above and opposite. *Transplanted from Australia to New Zealand almost 200 years ago, the black swan prospered to the point where hunting and egg harvests were necessary to control its numbers. On the South Island's Lake Ellesmere, the black swan population reached 100,000 before a storm in 1968 devastated critical feeding areas.* (Jean-Philippe Varin/ Jacana; Lynn M. Stone)

First overleaf. *Found from Texas to Argentina, black-bellied whistling ducks* (Dendrocygna autumnalis) *usually nest in tree cavities. When the young take to the water, they are closely guarded by both parents. In Central and South America, whistling-ducks are kept as watch-birds, for they protest loudly if disturbed.* (Larry R. Ditto)

Second overleaf. *The handsome mallard drake* (Anas platyrhynchos) *with its metallic green head is the world's most famous duck. Common everywhere in the Northern Hemisphere, the mallard is the ancestor of the white barnyard duck, and it may have been the first domesticated bird.* (Tim Fitzharris)

Opposite. *Churning the surface of a river, common mergansers (Mergus merganser) patter across the water to become airborne. All are adult drakes, which migrate separately from females and immatures. Ranging across North America and Eurasia, the common merganser—the name means "diving goose"—is the largest and most widespread of the so-called fish ducks. Sawlike ridges and a hooked tip on the bill enable these superb divers to feed on slippery prey. Tree cavities are the common merganser's favorite nest site. The ducklings—often a dozen or more— ride about on the mother's back.* (Guenter Ziesler)

Top. *A drake blue-winged teal (Anas discors) preens its handsome breeding plumage. This swift-flying little bird is the first duck to migrate in the fall, bound for wintering areas in Central and South America, and the last to return in spring.* (Wayne Lankinen)

Above. *On a bitterly cold winter morning, a drake redhead (Aythya americana) huddles on the ice fringing a Maryland estuary. Once the most abundant diving duck in North America, the redhead has suffered grievously from the conversion of its prairie wetland nesting areas to cropland.* (R.Y. Kaufman/Yogi, Inc.)

Right. *Southern Australia and Tasmania are home to the chestnut teal* (Anas castanea), *named for the drake's breeding colors. The male accompanies his mate and brood until the young have fledged, an uncommon trait among ducks.* (Anthony Mercieca)

Top two rows. *The plumage of most male ducks is brightly colored and boldly patterned, enabling the more soberly colored females to choose a mate of the right species. This helps to prevent hybridization among these closely related birds. Any bird that forms a pair with the wrong species will waste its energy, and its chance to contribute its genes to the next generation, because the hybrid young will almost certainly lack the adaptations—unique to each species—that enable these birds to survive. Instead, the young hybrids will have a mixture of adaptations, matching the needs of neither parent species.*

From the top row at the left to the bottom row at the right, the birds are a drake North American wood duck (Aix sponsa); *a Hottentot teal* (Anas punctata), *an African species in which the male and female look alike; a drake Baikal teal* (Anas formosa) *from eastern Asia; a drake Mandarin duck* (Aix galericulata), *also from eastern Asia; a female northern shoveler* (Anas clypeata), *a species found in North America and Eurasia; and a drake ringed teal* (Calonetta leucophrys) *from South America.* (Tim Zurowski; Anthony Mercieca, next two photos; Wayne Lankinen; Tim Fitzharris; Anthony Mercieca)

Overleaf. *Nearly every lake, pond, or pothole on the North American prairie has a breeding pair of blue-winged teal. The white crescent in front of the eye quickly identifies a male in breeding garb; both sexes have the pale blue shoulder patches that give this familiar dabbling duck its name. The hen incubates the seven to ten eggs in a down-lined hollow by the side of a pond; meanwhile the drake stands guard, poised on a stump or rock.* (Rod Planck)

Above and opposite. *Of the six species of saw-billed mergansers, only the smallest—the hooded merganser* (Lophodytes cucullatus)—*occurs exclusively in North America. This species catches fewer fish than other mergansers, preying instead on frogs, snails, and aquatic insects. The trademark of the male hooded merganser is a black-bordered white crest that is raised in dramatic fashion during aggression displays. By comparison, the female is rather drab, with a rust-orange crest. Hooded mergansers nest near wooded watercourses, darting through the trees with the skill of a fighter pilot.* (Tim Fitzharris)

Below. *Beating its loosely held wings against the water, a Dalmatian pelican (Pelecanus crispus) bathes on Lake Manyas in Turkey. This large, silvery-white pelican breeds from Yugoslavia to China and is a familiar winter visitor in India, but its numbers in southeast Europe have declined markedly in recent decades due to drainage of wetlands and persecution by fishermen. One study of Dalmatian pelicans estimated that two adult and two juvenile birds could eat 2,400 pounds of fish over an eight-month period.* (Guenter Ziesler)

Fishing with Pouches, Spears, and Hooks

The life of a fish isn't an easy one, and avoiding being eaten is of necessity a major preoccupation. Constant vigilance and surveillance are the wages of a watery existence, and escape into the center of a tight school helps reduce an individual's chance of becoming a meal. The difficulty of life as a fish is easily comprehended if you consider the diverse array of weaponry that can be marshalled by just a single group of piscivorous birds, the pelicans and their relatives.

The scooplike pouch is the most familiar distinguishing mark of the pelicans (family Pelecanidae), but this unusual and highly specialized feeding adaptation is but one of many shown by members of the order Pelecaniformes. The cormorants (family Phalacrocoracidae) pursue fish underwater, capturing them with hook-tipped bills, while their close relatives the anhingas, or darters (Anhingidae), spear fish with their thin, sharp, daggerlike bills. Boobies and gannets (family Sulidae) plunge into the water, often from great heights, to capture schooling fish near the surface; their sharp-edged, serrated bills ensure a tight hold on their prey. Tropicbirds (family Phaethontidae) feed over the open oceans, making ternlike plunges and dipping movements to the water's surface.

The distribution of these supreme fish-catchers coincides with the location of productive waters. Boobies, gannets, and the tropicbirds range far at sea; most cormorants are at home in coastal areas, while the anhingas and most of the pelicans live on estuarine or inland waters. The majority of species in this assemblage are partial to tropical or temperate regions, although the gannets and some cormorants occur in colder waters of the north and south.

Despite the outward diversity in their physical adaptations for feeding, the pelicans and their relatives share a number of features that set them apart from other groups of birds. Many water birds have webbed toes, but the pelican group is unique in having all four toes—rather than just three—connected by webbing. The legs are short and strong, and nearly all

81

members of the group are strong swimmers. The short legs and fully webbed toes represent an evolutionary compromise; on land, members of the order reveal, at best, a lack of grace.

Every child is familiar with the pouched throat of a pelican, but this area of bare skin, known as the gular pouch, is also seen in cormorants, boobies, and anhingas; among the Pelecaniformes, only the tropicbirds lack a gular pouch. In some species, the pouch is highly colored during the breeding season, and it frequently plays a role in courtship and display. The fluttering of the pouch's moist skin by a rapid, repeated action of the tongue apparatus is an important means of cooling for overheated birds in this group, perhaps contributing to the success of many species in tropical regions. But in the seven species of pelicans, the pouch has also become a critical component in a distinctive feeding apparatus.

Pelicans are found in warmer coastal regions and inland lakes nearly worldwide, though rarely will more than one or two species be found in a given area. The brown pelican (*Pelecanus occidentalis*) is a familiar bird of the coasts and offshore islands of the Caribbean and Pacific shores of the Americas; in its strictly marine way of life, it is not a typical pelican. Brown pelicans, including the large "Chilean" birds of the Humboldt Current off western South America, are the only pelicans that plunge-dive into the water, and flocks at work in productive fishing waters often make quite a splash. Idling on pier pilings, flying in silent, graceful lines over the ocean surface, or plunging in a fishing frenzy, brown pelicans are favorite characters in our coastal scenes. Yet in the middle decades of this century, their population suffered a serious decline as a result of accumulating pesticide residues. The near extinction of these birds taught us much about the threat that toxins pose in our environment; in recent years, the brown pelican's recovery in local areas has given rise to guarded optimism for a wiser future.

The other pelican species are predominantly white, and they include some of the largest flying birds. All use their huge, scooplike bills to catch fish in shallow coastal areas, both saltwater and fresh; some, such as the American and Eurasian white pelicans (*Pelecanus erythrorhynchos* and *P. onocrotalus*), perform their fishing in cooperative groups. Heavy and ungainly as they appear, pelicans are accomplished soarers, light-boned and long-winged. From a laborious take-off to their disappearance high into the sky as gleaming specks, white pelicans in wheeling flight provide a dazzling display of grace aloft. Most pelican species nest colonially, each pair raising one to three young. As in all pelecaniform birds except the tropicbirds, the young hatch helpless and naked, and must rely on their parents for many weeks.

The boobies and gannets represent the highest standard in the art of plunge-diving. These somewhat comical-looking birds sport sharply pointed bills with serrated edges, with which to grab fish underwater; the reduced gular pouch may help these birds to swallow large prey.

Gannets sometimes begin their dives more than a hundred feet above the sea; plunging straight down, they may send up a splash twelve feet high. A short underwater pursuit follows, and the catch is usually swallowed whole while the bird is still below the water's surface. There are three closely related species of gannets, all living in comparatively cold waters: the northern gannet (*Morus bassanus*), of the North Atlantic; the Cape gannet (*Morus capensis*), from the coasts of southern Africa; and the Australian gannet (*Morus serrator*).

Travelers to tropical oceans often encounter a wheeling, dipping flock of terns—and among them boobies, one after another, plunging forcefully but with smooth accuracy after the schooling fish below. The prey, flying fish in particular, are often driven near the surface by large predatory fish such as tuna, or disturbed by passing ships. Boobies differ from gannets only in minor respects. They are primarily birds of tropical and subtropical marine waters, although the Peruvian booby (*Sula variegata*) is limited to the relatively cold, highly productive waters of the Humboldt Current.

Perhaps the most abundant of the boobies is the red-footed (*Sula sula*), a small species that is highly variable in plumage, but whose adults are always easily recognized by their brilliant red feet. Red-footed boobies nest in trees or shrubs on tropical islands and range widely at sea to feed. The prosperity of a booby colony is closely tied to the abundance of fish and squid; anomalous oceanographic events, such as the warming of surface temperatures by the current called *El Niño*, may result in massive temporary breeding failures.

The most unusual booby, which may be only distantly related to the other boobies and gannets, is Abbott's booby (*Sula abbotti*). This species is now found only in forest trees on Christmas Island, off Java in the Indian Ocean, and its population is estimated at just 650 pairs. Although its tree-nesting habit makes it less vulnerable to introduced predators than many other island-nesters, Abbott's booby has suffered because of deforestation and phosphate mining.

In ethereal white plumage, winging over blue seas in strong direct flight, and trailing two improbably long tail streamers, the tropicbirds are a unique trio of seabirds. They are well known to sailors of the tropical oceans, who call them "bo'sun birds." The tropicbirds are highly oceanic members of the pelican assemblage, coming ashore only to nest. In the air, they move fluidly, but on land they are ungainly, even downright incompetent. Their greatly reduced legs allow no walking, and they must push themselves along the ground on their bellies. Poor walking ability does not adversely affect primarily aerial and aquatic birds such as the tropicbirds, and they gain an aerodynamic advantage by the reduction of the hind limbs.

Like boobies, tropicbirds plunge-dive for fish and squid. At sea they are generally solitary, but around breeding islands they chase, court, and display in groups, uttering shrill calls. Their aerial courtship involves graceful parallel glides and swoops.

The long tail streamers are white in the red-billed and white-tailed tropicbirds (*Phaethon aethereus* and *P. lepturus*) but red and stiff in the red-tailed tropicbird (*Phaethon rubricauda*); when resting on the water, the birds hold the streamers high, but move them rhythmically during courtship flights.

Numbering thirty-four species, the cormorants are perhaps the most highly adapted foot-propelled diving birds on earth. Their dives begin at the water's surface with a quick forward flip, and their underwater chases may last a minute or more. The long, flexible neck and straight, hook-tipped bill aid in capturing fish, while the stiff tail serves as a rudder. Because their plumage lacks the water-repellent property that most other seabirds have, cormorants are less buoyant and capable of more efficient underwater locomotion. Once out of the water, these birds must dry their wings; a still, black bird, its wings outstretched as it perches on a rock, piling, or buoy, is a familiar sight to many.

Most species of cormorants are coastal, nesting on cliffs or offshore islets and feeding in bays, estuaries, or inshore marine waters; certain species of the colder southern oceans nest in huge colonies where guano production has been exploited commercially for fertilizers. Two American species occur widely on inland waters: the more northerly double-crested cormorant (*Phalacrocorax auritus*) and the more tropical olivaceous cormorant (*Phalacrocorax olivaceus*). Several Old World species also occur locally on inland lakes and marshes, building stick nests in trees.

Among the modern pelecaniform birds, flightlessness has evolved only in the cormorants. The flightless cormorant (*Phalacrocorax harrisi*) occurs only on the Galapagos Islands; its reduced wings have a tattered look, and its strong feet, which provide propulsion underwater, allow only a tentative shuffling and hopping gait ashore.

Unique offshoots of the cormorants are the anhingas (*Anhinga*), odd-looking birds known variously also as darters, water-turkeys, or snake-birds. Anhingas do not have a hooked bill, but instead a slender and sharp-pointed one. They spear fish quickly, their rapid underwater thrusts aided by a special hinge mechanism in the neck vertebrae. Like cormorants, anhingas are "sinkers," and they often swim with only their heads and necks above the surface. They are found in tropical and subtropical freshwater and coastal swamp habitats; three species occur in the Old World, and one related form in the New World. Excellent soarers, they have long tails that give them a hawklike appearance in the air.

These, then, are the tools of the trade for the pelecaniform birds: spears, pouches, and hooks. In diversity, this array of fishing tackle rivals the ingenious inventions of fishermen. And in efficiency, over thousands of years of evolutionary time, the pelicans and their allies have proven themselves far superior to the most expert angler.

Opposite. *A brown pelican* (Pelecanus occidentalis) *begins its dive into a school of fish in the Sea of Cortez off Baja California. Cruising twenty to fifty feet above the waves, this saltwater pelican will suddenly plunge on half-folded wings, striking the water with its air-cushioned breast, and bobbing to the surface like a cork. The spectacular impact, which can be heard a half-mile away, stuns fish that are scooped up in the bird's throat pouch. The smallest of the pelicans, distinguished from its relatives by its dark plumage, this New World species nonetheless has a wingspan of up to seven and a half feet.* (François Gohier)

Overleaf. *In an elaborate presentation of nesting material, a male brown pelican relieves his mate at a desert island colony in the Sea of Cortez. These adaptable birds nest on sand or rocks on treeless islands, but build sturdy tree nests on mangrove-lined shores. North American brown pelican populations were decimated when pesticides accumulated from contaminated fish caused them to lay thin-shelled and easily broken eggs. The total failure of breeding colonies to produce young birds in southern California was traced to pollution from a single factory manufacturing* DDT. (C. Allan Morgan)

Opposite. *In breeding season, a three-inch-high plate grows on the upper bill of the American white pelican* (Pelecanus erythrorhynchos). *Like the antlers of deer, which are discarded after the rut, these plates fall off before the pelicans leave their northern prairie-lake nesting islands for warm wintering waters on the Gulf of Mexico. Despite their immense size and awkward efforts to become airborne, they are graceful fliers, and one of nature's spectacular sights is a flock of white pelicans circling high in a cloudless sky on black-tipped wings that span ten feet, then descending in an abrupt and thunderous dive.* (Steven C. Wilson/Entheos)

Above. *Bills agape like dip nets, Eurasian white pelicans* (Pelecanus onocrotalus) *encircle fish they have driven into the shallows by beating the water with their giant wings. Cooperative feeding, with long lines of swimming pelicans herding fish toward shore in army fashion, is typical of all but the brown pelican, the only member of the family to dive after its food. Once a pelican's pouch—which can hold up to three gallons of water and fish—is drained by tipping the bill downward, the bird swallows its catch. Young pelicans feed on partially digested fish by burying their heads in the parent's gullet.* (Frederic/Jacana)

Top two rows. *Beside a marshy slough in Florida's Everglades National Park, a male anhinga* (Anhinga anhinga) *grapples with a red-bellied turtle* (Chrysemys nelsoni) *that has been sunning itself in peace until the arrival of this long-necked relative of the cormorants. Fortunately, the turtle's shell is more than enough to protect it from the anhinga's sharp bill. After enduring several minutes of tapping and probing, the turtle heads for the water, and the frustrated anhinga begins preening itself as if nothing has happened.* (François Gohier)

Left. *Another male has better luck with a sunfish, the sort of prey its bill enables it to deal with.* (Gay Bumgarner/Photo/Nats)

Opposite. *The symmetry of a colony of imperial shags (*Phalacrocorax atriceps) *on the Argentine coast is remarkable and intentional. Each nest—a lump of seaweed plastered together with offal and guano—is situated just out of reach of neighboring birds. Like all cormorant chicks, those of the imperial shag are born blind and naked, and in their first helpless days the parent birds drop bits of half-digested food into their maws. Later, they will fish their meals out of the adults' gullets.* (François Gohier)

Above. *To dry their waterlogged flight feathers, cormorants come ashore and spread their wings to the sun. Through evolution, the wings of the flightless cormorant (*Phalacrocorax harrisi) *of the Galapagos Islands were long ago reduced to mere stubs. But the wing-drying behavior was retained, producing one of the strangest sights in the natural world. The bird's size, together with an unusually strong beak, waterproof body plumage that is unique in the family, and the disappearance of the burdensome flight feathers, enable the flightless cormorant to remain submerged for long periods.* (Rudolf Konig/Jacana)

Opposite. *Newly arrived at their nesting colony off the coast of Scotland, a pair of northern gannets* (Morus bassanus) *performs a courtship ceremony in which the birds briefly turn their heads away from one another, displaying the golden-yellow of the nape. Gannets can be seen perched on rocks only during the breeding season. They spend the rest of the year at sea, where the handsome, gleaming-white plumage of the adults is visible for over a mile. Sometimes these goose-sized seabirds can be seen gathered over a school of fish, plunging into the waves in pursuit of their prey.* (Hans D. Dossenbach)

Above. *One of a half-dozen New World breeding sites for the northern gannet, Bird Island is a sheer-sided spire of rock only a stone's throw away from the mainland of Newfoundland. Its rounded top is covered with closely packed gannet nests, each one a pile of seaweed and excrement just out of reach of its neighbors. With much jabbing of bills, a pair of gannets defends its nest for three months, until the single chick is old enough to leave the colony.* (Joy Spurr)

Top two rows and left. *A colony of blue-footed boobies* (Sula nebouxii) *at the height of breeding activity bustles with marvelous courtship, greeting, and territorial displays. Birds parade about with cocked tails, lifting their gaudy webbed feet high off the ground with great deliberation. Sky-pointing, saluting, bill-jabbing, wing-rattling, symbolic nest-building, and even aerial flashing of those ridiculously colored feet—all are necessary to the production of a new generation. Blue-footed boobies nest on tropical and subtropical islands off the Pacific coast of Central and South America, from Mexico to Peru.* (Karl H. Switak; Hans D. Dossenbach)

Overleaf. *A "lively twig-hopper" is how one seabird authority described the red-footed booby* (Sula sula). *Because it nests in trees rather than on the ground, as gannets and other boobies do, the red-footed booby has short legs and walks with difficulty. Instead, evolution has given it feet that are flexible and prehensile, for grasping branches on its tropical nesting islands.* (Dale and Marian Zimmerman)

Below. *Common murres (Uria aalge), each brooding a single egg, appear evenly spaced on a narrow nesting ledge carved by waves from a seaward cliff. There is little room to spare in murre colonies, which may number as many as 75,000 breeding pairs, and bitter fights erupt if a bird lands on the wrong ledge. Murres lay their eggs on bare rock, and observers have long believed that the egg's pear shape would prevent it from rolling over the edge if dislodged. However, scientists studying murres in the Canadian Arctic say that many eggs fall off anyway, and suggest that the egg is shaped to conform to the incubating bird's body.*
(Jean-Paul Ferrero/Auscape International)

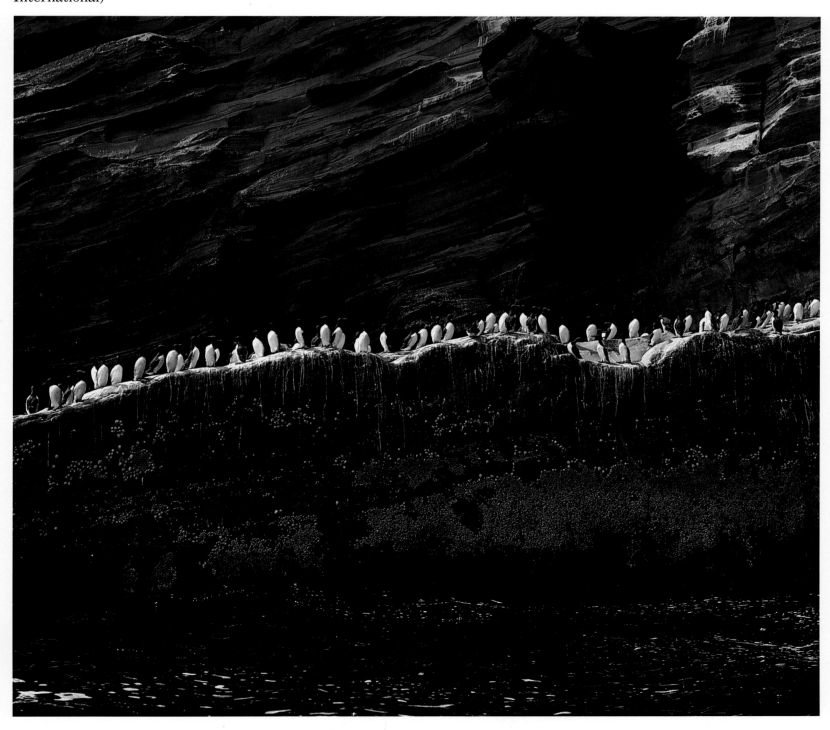

Cliff Dwellers of the North

The cliffs of St. Paul Island rise almost vertically from the icy gray waters of the Bering Sea, some 300 miles from the mainland of Alaska. Such a cold and forbidding spot would seem unlikely to produce any excitement for bird watchers . . . or for birds. Yet every year, during the brief subarctic summer, the cliffs of St. Paul come alive with a remarkable avian spectacle, as literally millions of seabirds come to nest.

The noisy throngs on the rocks include three kinds of gulls, a cormorant, and that stubby albatross in miniature, the northern fulmar (*Fulmarus glacialis*). But the real stars of the show on St. Paul are members of the Alcidae, the auk family. This group includes various murres, puffins, guillemots, murrelets, and auklets, plus the razorbill (*Alca torda*) and the dovekie (*Alle alle*). For convenience, bird watchers and scientists usually refer to all these birds collectively as "alcids."

Around the rocky perimeter of the island, alcids are never out of sight. On the ledges of the higher rock faces stand rows of murres, their upright posture and elegant black-and-white pattern somewhat reminiscent of penguins. Where piles of boulders line the beach, swarms of tiny least auklets (*Aethia pusilla*) fly to and fro or perch on the rocks, making chirring sounds like starlings. On softer soil near the tops of the cliffs, horned puffins and tufted puffins (*Fratercula corniculata* and *F. cirrhata*) turn their clownlike faces this way and that to peer at the approaching observer. Groups of parakeet auklets (*Cyclorrhynchus psittacula*) and tight flocks of crested auklets (*Aethia cristatella*) fly low over the sea, swing up past the cliffs, and then veer away again. This is a spectacle of abundance, and all of these alcids find food for themselves and their young in the waters around the island.

Alcids fly very well—underwater. If we watch a flock of auklets swimming just offshore, we may see them suddenly dive: not all at once, but in rapid succession, each one abruptly throwing its head forward and down, up-ending as it goes down headfirst. A sharp eye will notice that each bird flips its wings open as it goes under, so that the last we see of the disappearing alcid is its short, pointy tail and, off to each side, the tip of each wing. The birds "fly" underwater with their wings almost fully spread. Their broad, webbed feet may be spread out to help with steering, but not to help push.

Clearly the wing power of the alcids is highly effective for travel beneath the surface. Most of them find all of their food underwater. The smaller auklets feed upon tiny, shrimplike crustaceans, abundant in these northern waters; the puffins and murres, for the most part, catch small fish. Some of the larger alcids are known to hunt for food more than 500 feet below the surface. All of these little living submarines are quite successful at feeding because they have power, speed, and great maneuverability underwater.

Alcids in the air, however, are not so impressive. Long wings would be a hindrance underwater, so evolution has made their wings short and strong instead. Taking off from the water, many alcids have to splash along the surface until they build up enough speed to become airborne. Once in the air, they have to flap their wings very fast, and some of the smaller kinds tend to veer back and forth in flight, as if they were having some trouble in steering.

Nevertheless, these birds are able to disperse from the colony to find food enough for all. Murres at some Canadian nesting sites sometimes fly fifty miles or more from their colonies to do their fishing. The birds on St. Paul probably have no need to travel so far; in fact, just forty miles away is another island, St. George, with millions more alcids. These cold northern seas are actually teeming with underwater life, and the alcids are perfectly adapted to take advantage of this bounty. They fly over the seas to reach new feeding areas, "fly" beneath the surface to catch their food, and then fly up to the safety of their nesting sites on the cliffs.

The life-style of the alcids is clearly a successful one. For proof of that, we need only consider how numerous some of them have become. The thick-billed murre (*Uria lomvia*), the dovekie, and the least auklet may be the three most abundant water birds in the northern hemisphere, each with a total population running into the tens of millions.

Seen in winter, the members of this family do not seem like a very diverse lot. If you visit a place where these birds can be seen from shore in winter, such as Point Pinos in California or the outer arm of Cape Cod in Massachusetts, you will understand why the generic term "alcid" is so necessary: in winter, these birds all look alike. All are gray or blackish above and whitish below, with minor variations and size differences that are difficult to judge over the open ocean.

But these birds are anything but drab in summer. The breeding season is, after all, the time of year when they must be able to recognize one another; and most of the alcids advertise their identities by putting on gaudy faces in summer.

The clowns of St. Paul Island are the tufted puffin and the horned puffin, marked by their big triangular bills, brightly patterned with red and yellow. The tufted puffin is known by the long, drooping, blond tufts of feathers on its head in summer. The horned puffin has a short fleshy "horn" above each eye, but otherwise looks much like the Atlantic puffin (*Fratercula arctica*), which is common in parts of eastern Canada and extends south to some islands off the coast of Maine, as well as on the coasts of Scandinavia and the British Isles. All puffins are fish-eaters; they may be seen flying to their nesting burrows carrying half a dozen fish crosswise in their huge bills.

The three kinds of auklets on St. Paul also have fancy faces during the nesting season. The diminutive least auklet is the least decorative, developing only tiny white filaments or plumes on its forehead and face. These plumes may be all the auklets need to see at close range, but the human observer is likely to be more impressed with the great variability in the birds' overall pattern. Some least auklets in summer are heavily marked with gray on the underparts, while others are nearly white below; no two individuals in a flock look quite the same, and this variability tends to give the species a dowdy or unfinished look.

More elegant are the other two auklet species here, the parakeet auklet and the crested auklet. Both have slaty-gray heads with a white streak behind the eye, and in summer their bills are bright waxy-red, shaped so as to suggest an exaggerated smile. In addition, the crested sports a curly topknot on its forehead, curving forward over its bill.
The most ornate of the auklets in the Bering Sea is not found on St. Paul, and in fact it is rather rare and poorly known. The whiskered auklet (*Aethia pygmaea*) nests on only a few islands in the Aleutian chain. Few visitors to Alaska get to see this striking bird, with its long gray crest and three long white plumes on each side of its head.

South of the Bering Sea, nesting on islands along both sides of the North Pacific, the rhinoceros auklet (*Cerorhinca monocerata*) lives up to its name by developing an erect "horn" at the base of its bill during the breeding season. It also sports two white plumes on its face at this time. Some of the island colonies of "rhinos" are quite large, but unlike many northern alcid colonies, they present no great spectacle for the observer. Rhinoceros auklets nest in underground burrows, like puffins, and they visit their colonies only at night.

Two small alcids of the Pacific, the marbled and Kittlitz's murrelets (*Brachyramphus marmoratus* and *B. brevirostris*) seem to reverse the usual family rule of wearing their brightest patterns in summer. These two murrelets are rather attractively marked in black and white during the winter, but for the breeding season they molt into a drab plumage of mottled brown. There is a reason for this: they need the camouflage. Unlike alcids that nest in large colonies in the safety of isolated islands, these two murrelets nest as scattered pairs on large islands and on the mainland, where predators abound. It pays for these murrelets to be as inconspicuous as possible when they are on land.

In fact, the marbled murrelet has carried inconspicuousness to a remarkable extreme. Even though the bird is common along the coast from southern Alaska to northern California, no one managed to find a nest in North America until 1974! The discovery itself was rather bizarre, as the nest was found by a tree surgeon trimming branches in a Douglas-fir over a campground in California. The murrelet's nest was a clump of moss on a branch 150 feet above the ground. If these small alcids always nest high in trees in dense coniferous forests, and fly to and from their nests only at night, it is no wonder they are not detected there more often.

Many scientists believe that the alcid family must have had its beginnings in the North Pacific or the Bering Sea, because eighteen of the twenty-two species of alcids occur there, while only six are found in the North Atlantic. Those six are quite common, however. The smallest, the dovekie, feeds along the edges of the pack ice and breeds by the millions in the high arctic regions of the Atlantic.

Studies in eastern Canada have suggested that the larger alcids are capable of astoundingly deep dives. While the slender black guillemot (*Cepphus grylle*) apparently goes no deeper than about 170 feet and the chunky Atlantic puffin barely reaches 200 feet, the razorbill can get down to 400 feet, and the common murre (*Uria aalge*) can dive to nearly 600 feet below the surface. If this pattern holds, the deepest diver of them all might have been the great auk (*Pinguinus impennis*), now extinct. This big bird, standing more than two feet tall— nearly twice the size of any living alcid—was once common in parts of the North Atlantic.

The evolutionary trade-off for the great auk's size was that it had lost the ability to fly. Superb though it may have been as a swimmer, it could not fly up to the safety of the cliffside nesting sites occupied by its smaller cousins. Great auks nested only on a few low, relatively flat islands where they could scramble up out of the surf; these islands were free of predators—until man arrived. Sailors who discovered these nesting islands found they could club down the auks by the hundreds. Eventually the great bird was driven to extinction.

Yet we are left with a curious reminder of their passing. European sailors had long referred to the great auk as "pinguin" or "pengwyn," or variations on such a name, the origin of which is debated. Later, when European explorations had extended well into the Southern Hemisphere, sailors rounding the tip of southern Africa saw birds that looked much like great auks: black and white, standing upright on the island rocks, and unable to fly. Although these birds were not related to the auks, it was only natural that the sailors should call them "pengwyns" as well . . . and the name stuck. Today probably not one person in a hundred knows of the great auk, or mourns its loss, but everyone has heard of penguins.

Opposite. *Neatly garbed in black and white—a seabird in a tuxedo— the razorbill* (Alca torda) *is aptly named for its large, laterally flattened bill, crossed by a bold white stripe. Although there are a few large razorbill colonies in the North Atlantic, these birds tend to breed in small groups in the company of murres and puffins. The single egg is laid among boulders, in a rock crevice, or occasionally in an enlarged puffin burrow in the soft clifftop turf. Powerful swimmers, propelled by both wings and feet, razorbills pursue eel-like sand lance and small herringlike fish called sprat, which they carry live to their nestlings. Young razorbills leave their natal island when they are only three weeks old, fluttering to the sea on half-grown wings, and swimming and diving with inherent expertise.* (Jean-Paul Ferrero/Jacana)

Row above. *All but six of the twenty-two members of the auk clan are found only in the North Pacific, and do not occur in the Atlantic Ocean. Many biologists believe this is evidence that the family first evolved here, and only later spread into the Atlantic. The smallest auklets, the species that have red bills and head plumes, are concentrated in the Bering Sea and on the Aleutian Islands. The larger members of the family, including the puffinlike rhinoceros auklet that wears a whitish "horn" during the breeding season, nest both in the Bering Sea region and on rocky coasts farther to the south.*

From left to right, the species shown are the crested auklet (Aethia cristatella), *least auklet* (Aethia pusilla), *parakeet auklet* (Cyclorrhynchus psittacula), *rhinoceros auklet* (Cerorhinca monocerata), *whiskered auklet* (Aethia pygmaea), *and the pigeon guillemot* (Cepphus columba), *the most abundant species on the California coast.* (Art Wolfe; C. Gable Ray; Robert Y. Kaufman/Yogi, Inc; Kevin Schafer/Tom Stack and Associates; C. Fred Zeillemaker; Jeff Foott)

Above and opposite. *Puffed-up puffins or "sea parrots" are the most popular of all seabirds in the northern oceans. The horned puffin (Fratercula corniculata), with its red-and-yellow bill and fleshy black protuberances above each eye, nests in cliffside crevices on islands in the frigid waters of the North Pacific off Alaska and Siberia. The tufted puffin (Fratercula cirrhata), with its curving blond head plumes and orange-and-green bill, nests in burrows as far south as central California on the Pacific coast of North America, and to northern Japan on the coast of Asia.* (Art Wolfe; Leonard Lee Rue III)

Overleaf. *To waterproof its feathers, an Atlantic puffin (Fratercula arctica) tweaks an oil gland at the base of its tail, rubs the exuding grease onto its head, and then uses its head as an oily mop to swab the rest of its plumage. Puffin congregations usually appear peaceful, but fights do take place; despite slashing wings and savage wrenching of heads with formidable bills—which can draw blood from a human hand—the combatants are not usually seriously hurt. Puffins are generally silent, their only vocalization an infrequent growl— suggesting a chainsaw being started—uttered underground.* (Frank S. Todd)

Below. *Standing three feet tall and weighing thirty to forty pounds, the brightly colored king penguin (Aptenodytes patagonica) of sub-Antarctic islands is the second largest member of its clan. King penguins lay their eggs in summer, male and female sharing incubation chores for eight weeks. With their parents bringing them two pounds of fish and squid from nearby kelp beds every hour, the chicks add layers of fat until, by onset of winter, they weigh twenty-five pounds. But a third of their body weight will be lost during long fasts when the islands are buffeted by storms and the young penguins, huddled in their crèche, wait two weeks between meals.* (Frank S. Todd)

Of Rockhoppers and Kings

They form an eerie parade: big birds, standing upright more than three feet tall, shuffling silently over the ice. Behind them is the relative "warmth" of their usual surroundings, the Antarctic Ocean, where the water temperature cannot dip much below freezing; ahead lies the prospect of temperatures that can drop to seventy degrees below zero or colder. Across the ice they march, mile after mile. Here in the coldest region on earth, when the long, dark, Antarctic winter is coming on, the emperor penguins (*Aptenodytes forsteri*) are going to the place where they will nest and raise their young.

The emperor is the only penguin that goes to such extremes of masochism; the others at least raise their young during the comparative mildness of summer. Even so, most of the seventeen species of penguins live under conditions that seem harsh and difficult to us—in the cold seas and around the rocky islands and coasts of the Southern Hemisphere. But this is the niche that they have evolved to fill, and they are superbly designed for their unique style of life.

Penguins are the ultimate swimmers among birds, with a structure that has been highly modified for travel through the water. In the previous chapter we met the alcids of the Northern Hemisphere, rather penguinlike birds that make a compromise between using their wings for underwater travel and using them for flight in the air. Penguins make no such compromise: all are flightless. Their wings have been shortened, flattened, and stiffened until they hardly look like wings, and it seems more appropriate to think of them as flippers.

The body of a penguin is shaped like a torpedo, streamlined for smooth travel through the water, and the feet are placed far back on the body and used as rudders for underwater steering. While most birds have hollow bones, to make them lighter in weight for easier flight, penguins have solid bones: it is useful for the birds to be as heavy as possible when they are heading for deeper levels. The emperor penguin, largest member of the family, is known to reach depths of more than 850 feet below the surface, and it can stay underwater for up to nine minutes at a time.

Seen from a ship at sea, penguins might be mistaken for porpoises at first, because they often swim in the same way—with a series of shallow leaps above the surface—unlike any other birds. Indeed, early travelers to the southern oceans debated whether penguins were birds or fish or mammals.

Besides being built for swimming, several kinds of penguins are also adapted to survive conditions of extraordinary cold. The feathers of these birds are small and hard, and are placed very densely over their bodies; even at close range, they look more like scales than feathers. The birds also have a layer of fine downy plumes between the skin and the outer coat of feathers, and thick layers of fat just below the skin, so that they are quite well insulated.

There is one distinct advantage to the penguins' cold world: food is abundant in the icy waters of the Southern Hemisphere. Some of the larger penguins, and those found farthest away from the South Pole, feed on small squids and fish. Many of the smaller and medium-sized penguins feed on the tiny shrimplike creatures known collectively as "krill." The abundance of this food source is suggested by the fact that it also supports the big baleen whales, which strain the krill from the water with the strips of whalebone, or baleen, in their mouths. These gentle giants were once very common in the southern oceans, until commercial whaling depleted their numbers; there always was, and still is, plenty of krill to feed thousands of huge whales and millions of penguins.

Most penguins are sociable creatures. They are usually seen in groups, although they tend to mix only with their own kind, and not with other species of penguins. Their gregarious nature is especially noticeable during the nesting season, when they gather into large colonies, or "penguin cities."

Among the largest nesting colonies in the Antarctic are those of the Adelie penguins (*Pygoscelis adeliae*), the black-and-white dwarfs that probably come closest to the public stereotype of what penguins should look like. Colonies of Adelies may run into the tens of thousands, or even hundreds of thousands. They lay their eggs and raise their young on the bare soil and gravel of the Antarctic continent and nearby islands, using the same sites year after year.

In early spring, when the first Adelies come to the colonies, they may have to walk across many miles of ice that has not yet broken up. The first to arrive are all males, each intent on laying claim to a small patch of ground that will be the nesting territory. Having staked his claim, usually after a great deal of squabbling with other males on all sides, each waits for the females to arrive, as they will within a matter of days.

Prospecting for mates, male Adelie penguins advertise themselves by pointing their bills straight up in the air, waving their flippers about, and making loud gargling sounds.

Evidently female Adelies find this very attractive, because pairs form quickly. Most of the time the birds will choose the same mates year after year, and it might seem remarkable that in the huge colonies, among thousands of look-alikes, two individuals would be able to find each other. Actually, they are responding partly to location—the males tend to establish precisely the same territories each year if they can—and partly to their ability to recognize each other by voice. Each bird has plenty of opportunity to hear its partner's voice: members of a pair have a display in which they stand facing each other and wave their heads back and forth in the air, calling loudly. This display evidently helps to strengthen the pair bond between the two.

In most of the places where Adelies nest, no conventional nest-building material is available, so their nests are simply collections of small stones. The birds may go to considerable effort to gather these pebbles, often stealing them from the nests of their neighbors.

After the stony nest of each Adelie pair is completed, the female lays two eggs there, and then she goes back to the sea. By this time she is undoubtedly hungry: the process of coming ashore, going through courtship, and laying the eggs usually has taken more than two weeks, and penguins do not feed on land, only at sea. The male is probably hungry too, but he has not had the great energy demand of laying the eggs; so he takes the first turn at incubating them. The female stays away feeding for about two weeks, and then she takes a two-week turn incubating while the male goes to get his long-awaited breakfast in the ocean. Some time after the male returns to begin his second shift, the eggs hatch into fuzzy, rotund little penguin chicks.

For the next month the parents must continue to take turns, one guarding the young and keeping them warm, the other fishing for krill, which will be brought back and regurgitated for the chicks. When the baby penguins are not quite so helpless, all the young in the neighborhood gather into a little herd, or crèche, where they can be guarded by just a few adults while all the rest of the parents go out foraging for food. A returning adult can recognize its own offspring (and vice versa) by voice. The parent Adelies will continue to feed their young for some two months, but in later stages the feedings become less and less frequent; finally, hunger may drive the young into the ocean to fend for themselves.

Although the nesting cycle of the Adelie serves as a good introduction to the habits of penguins in general, each of the other sixteen species has its own special variations.

At the beginning of this chapter we met the emperor penguin, the only bird to go through the peak of its nesting activity during the frigid blackness of the Antarctic winter. Since the emperor's nesting colonies are usually on solid ice, we might wonder how they could possibly incubate their eggs: while the bird warmed one side of the egg, wouldn't the other side be frozen against the ice? But the bird has a remarkable solution:

the incubating penguin places the egg on top of its large feet and covers it with a loose fold of belly skin, so that the egg is surrounded by warmth. This habit is shared by a close relative, the king penguin (*Aptenodytes patagonica*), which lives in a slightly milder climate in the sub-Antarctic and nests during the summer.

The six species of crested penguins, marked by their decorative head plumes of yellow or orange, are characteristic of the sub-Antarctic—the regions just outside the belt of coldest water. The smallest and most widespread member of this group is the rockhopper penguin (*Eudyptes crestatus*). There are millions of rockhoppers on the Falkland Islands, millions more on islands in the southern Indian Ocean, nesting in huge and noisy colonies where the birds seem to be bickering constantly. The name comes from the bird's habit of jumping ("bouncing" might be a better word) from one boulder to another as it travels about the rocky islands where it nests. Going back to the sea, diving into the water, most penguins dive in headfirst, but the rockhopper jumps in feetfirst.

Four of the crested penguins have rather limited ranges on islands near New Zealand, but the remaining species, the macaroni penguin (*Eudyptes chrysolophus*), is widespread on the Antarctic Peninsula and on islands in the southern Atlantic and Indian oceans. The odd name of this bird originated with the fact that "macaroni" was a slang term for fashionable dandies in eighteenth-century England. Early travelers who encountered these penguins must have felt that the birds' facial plumes looked like a caricature of high fashion.

Another distinctive group includes the four species known as the "jackass penguins" because of their loud, braying voices. All have black chest bands and black-and-white patterns on their faces. The original jackass penguin (*Spheniscus demersus*) is found off the coasts of southern Africa, while the other three—the Magellanic, Humboldt, and Galapagos penguins (*Spheniscus magellanicus*, *S. humboldti*, and *S. mendiculus*)—inhabit the waters around South America. These are all burrowing penguins; they dig nesting tunnels in the soil, but if the soil is too hard for digging, they find some sort of small depression or shelter.

Penguins are so routinely thought of as birds of the polar zone that it is hard to remember that one species actually lives on the Equator. This is the Galapagos penguin, one of the smallest and rarest members of the family. Although the Galapagos Islands are bathed by a cold ocean current that flows up along the western side of South America, the water temperature here is still usually above sixty degrees Fahrenheit, a far cry from the freezing waters where penguins like the emperor and the Adelie thrive.

In our glimpses of penguin life-styles on land, at the varied places where they come ashore to nest, we may find them amazing or amusing. But it is only when they return to the sea that they come into their own as the ultimate swimming birds.

Opposite, first and second overleaves. *The emperor penguin* (Aptenodytes forsteri) *is the only bird that does not breed on land or use a nest of any kind. Four feet tall and weighing up to ninety pounds, the largest of all penguins breeds instead on the Antarctic sea ice in the dead of winter.*
Emperors assemble in their colonies during March, as the icepack begins to form. Once the female lays her single egg, she walks back to the open sea, which may now be sixty miles distant. For two months the male moves awkwardly about, balancing the egg on his feet and insulating it with a blanket of skin. Huddling with thousands of other males for warmth, he lives off his fat reserve until shortly before the egg hatches, when his mate returns and feeds the hatchling. Then male and female take turns brooding the chick on their feet and making foraging trips.
In a few weeks, the young penguin leaves its parents' feet and huddles with other chicks, freeing both adults for shuttle service to the ever-closer shoreline. When the icepack breaks up in December, the emperors drift northward on the ice floes—a unique mode of migration. (J. Prevost/Jacana, first two photos; Frank S. Todd)

Third overleaf. *Everyone's favorite penguin, and the one that has inspired thousands of cartoons of tuxedo-clan birds, is the Adelie penguin* (Pygoscelis adeliae). *Adelies live by the millions in colonies that rim the frozen Antarctic continent. Here a crowd of Adelies approaches the shore, preparing to go to sea in pursuit of krill—tiny crustaceans that live in the cold ocean waters of the Southern Hemisphere.* (Frank S. Todd)

Opposite and above. *Whenever a group of Adelie penguins leaves a colony and is about to enter the water to feed, there is a certain amount of hesitation. The birds are reluctant to enter the water because a voracious leopard seal (*Hydrurga leptonyx) *might be present. Finally, after much crowding and jostling, one of the birds at the edge of the ice is pushed over, and the rest of the penguins promptly follow in a cascade of quick dives, trying to confuse the dangerous predator with a shower of targets.* (Art Wolfe; Frank S. Todd)

Above and left. *Leopard seals patrol the shoreline at Adelie rookeries, often following companies of birds on their way back to the colony after a fishing expedition. Singling out a bird porpoising toward home, a seal drops beneath the icy surface to ambush its prey from below. A leopard seal can swim faster than a penguin, and while an Adelie may find temporary respite in dodges and sudden turns, the seal will pursue a penguin until the bird is exhausted.* (Frank S. Todd)

Above and opposite. *Pursued by seals, a group of Adelie penguins vaults vertically out of the water, landing feetfirst atop ice cakes twice their height above the sea. Scientists watching Adelie rookeries believe that leopard seals claim five percent of the breeding population during the nesting season.* (Frank S. Todd)

First overleaf. *A female Adelie lays one or two eggs in a nest of small stones, and then leaves to feed at sea while the male incubates the eggs. Two weeks later the female returns and the male goes to sea. At seven weeks of age, the young shed their downy coats and then resemble the adults.* (Gary Strassler/Amwest)

Second overleaf. *A triangular white patch over the eye is the badge of the gentoo penguin (Pygoscelis papua). Well-worn paths lead from the sea to the rookeries of "Johnny" penguins on the tussocky islands that ring the Antarctic Ocean. Young gentoo penguins are fed a diet of regurgitated shrimp; the stomach of one gentoo held the remains of 960 crustaceans.* (François Gohier)

Opposite. *Squid and cuttlefish are staples in the diet of the Magellanic penguin* (Spheniscus magellanicus), *which nests in burrows on the Falkland Islands and from Cape Horn north along the coast of Patagonia. To lay their two white eggs, Magellanic penguins tunnel up to ten feet into sand dunes, peat, coastal bluffs, or woodland turf; the nest is a mound of feathers, leaves, and pebbles. Some of the people who live along the Strait of Magellan kill large numbers of this piebald penguin for its skin.* (Art Wolfe)

Above. *Like its relative the Magellanic penguin, the jackass penguin* (Spheniscus demersus), *shown here quietly entering the water, uses its strong bill to dig nesting burrows in the sand. Named for its braying call, this two-foot penguin inhabits bleak islands off the South African coast. Nesting on guano islands in the cold ocean off Chile and Peru, Humboldt penguins* (Spheniscus humboldti) *feed on anchovies. This is the most endangered penguin, its numbers reduced mainly because of mining operations in the guano deposits it needs for its burrows.* (Charles G. Summers, Jr./Amwest; Anthony Mercieca)

Overleaf. *The yellow-eyed penguin (Megadyptes antipodes) lurks in the mossy shadows of stunted forests on New Zealand's South Island and the nearby Aucklands. Two chicks will be reared in an isolated nook under roots or a log. Intensive studies of the yellow-eyed penguin show that females begin to breed at an age of two years, but these young birds meet with limited success; only thirty-two percent of the two-year-olds hatch eggs, compared with seventy-eight percent for three-year-olds and ninety-five percent for fully mature, four-year-old females.*

The failed nesting attempts by younger females are nonetheless viewed as a valuable learning experience. Yellow-eyed penguins remain in the area year-round, feeding on squid and small fish and coming ashore at night. (Fred Bruemmer)

Above. *The acrobatic and agile rockhopper penguin (Eudyptes crestatus) gets around by jumping from boulder to boulder, keeping its balance with the aid of sharp claws. This two-foot-tall crested penguin lives on temperate islands around Antarctica, and some of its colonies are enormous; one small island near the Falklands hosts between two and three million birds. Rockhopper penguins nest in caves, crevices, or on open stony terraces.* (Art Wolfe)

Opposite. *With their exquisite bright yellow plumes, macaroni penguins (Eudyptes chrysolophus) have a rather dandified appearance—hence the name. The macaroni nests on sub-Antarctic islands in the Atlantic and Indian oceans. The female macaroni penguin lays one to three eggs, which her mate incubates for the first three weeks, leaning into the buffeting winds at a forty-five-degree angle or even lying on his breast. Only one chick, however, is likely to survive. Visitors to macaroni penguin colonies are greeted by a powerful goatish smell.* (Art Wolfe)

Below. *Skuas excel as birds of prey, especially near penguin colonies. Here a brown skua (Catharacta skua) snatches a hapless gentoo penguin chick from a Falkland Islands rookery while its mate distracts the parent. Called the "Eagle of the South Pole" by one naturalist, this skua is the only one of the world's 9,100 birds to breed in the polar regions of both hemispheres. Like its gull relatives, this stout, dark-plumaged bird is an opportunistic scavenger—its name means "cleanser"—and is also skilled at harassing other seabirds into yielding their catch.* (Frank S. Todd)

Patrollers of Sea, Sky, and Shore

Close your eyes and plant your bare feet in the cool sands of an ocean shore. Breathe the salt-mist air and let your ears take note of your surroundings. The surf crashes offshore, then laps at the beach; this is the first thing you notice. And then the gulls cry, their mews and squeals playing off the roar of the waves. Some calls are guttural with a threatening edge; others sound like laughter. Gulls and the beach—an ancient alliance.

There is scarcely any water bird as storied, as familiar, and as associated with man as the "sea gull," a generic concept we have constructed which neither does justice to the fascinating variety of the world's gulls, nor accurately describes the gulls' realm. The gulls are just one of several closely related groups of birds that patrol the meeting of sky, sea, and land; there are also the terns, the jaegers and skuas, and the skimmers. These ninety-six species of birds form the family Laridae. And unrelated, but soaring the tropical coasts like out-sized gulls, are the frigatebirds, of the family Fregatidae, whose closest cousins are the pelecaniform birds we met earlier. Each of these groups of birds is fascinating itself, and they add up to much more than our simple notion of a sea gull.

The gulls and their relatives are long-winged, web-footed water birds adapted to a life patrolling the airspace over water, shore, and marsh. There is little that is outstandingly specialized in their external form, except for the long bills of the skimmers. But gulls and their relatives have molded a rather standard body shape into some remarkably successful machineries that have given them a foothold in nearly every wetland and coastal habitat on earth. As opportunists and scavengers, certain gulls are at home in the hearts of our largest cities; they forage at garbage dumps, trash-strewn schoolyards, or a fish-cleaning operation as readily as they might at a pristine shore or estuary. In contrast, the diminutive Ross' gull (*Rhodostethia rosea*) patrols Arctic shorelines and pack ice so remote from civilization that an individual straggler makes front-page news when it strays as far south as our northernmost big cities. During the breeding season, many gulls live far inland, defying the classic notion of the "sea gull"; certain terns, on the other hand, are highly pelagic—only the albatrosses and petrels have a more thoroughly oceanic existence.

Perhaps more than any other kind of bird, gulls give the lie to the notion that all members of a species look alike. There are about forty-five species of gulls in the world, occurring chiefly in temperate or colder latitudes. Plumage variation within a species can be staggering, a never-ending challenge, and at times a cause for consternation among bird watchers. A young gull's first plumage is known as its juvenal plumage; when it loses this garb—which is usually brown and mottled—a young gull takes from one to three more years to develop the fully adult plumage. During each of these years, immature gulls acquire a different plumage through a complete annual molt; to add to the complexity, there is often a partial molt in the spring that results in a summer plumage slightly different from the previous winter's. Many adult gulls have distinct breeding and nonbreeding plumages. Superimposed on this plumage and molt cycle is a geographic or "racial" variation in size and plumage that is often quite pronounced, as in the herring gull (*Larus argentatus*) and some of its close relatives. What is more, such factors as individual variation, hybridization, and plumage anomalies like albinism serve to increase further the already bewildering variety of plumages to be seen in a flock of gulls. The challenge of identification is there for the keen birder to tackle!

Many gull species lead a dual life, spending the breeding season in the interiors of the continents and migrating to the coasts for the remainder of the year. Thus the irony of a "sea gull"—the California gull (*Larus californicus*)—being honored as the state bird of landlocked Utah. An offshoot of the herring gull species group, the California gull evolved in the Great Basin region of western North America. Grasshoppers and other insects, brine shrimp of the basin's alkali lakes, small mammals, and bird's eggs form their summer diet; this contrasts with the fish and marine invertebrates and, more recently, the refuse of human society that sustain the same species through the winter months along the Pacific Coast. The gray gull (*Larus modestus*) of the coastal desert of Chile and Peru also nests inland, in one of the earth's most arid regions; but, unlike the California and other inland nesting gulls, it derives no sustenance from its desert nesting habitat. Instead, it enjoys relative freedom there from predators that abound on the coast, such as the larger kelp gull (*Larus dominicanus*). Gray gulls must commute twenty miles or more to the coast to feed, and of course they must also cope with the extreme temperatures in their desert nesting colonies; but their strategy has proven a successful one.

About half of the world's gull species are found in marine habitats throughout the year, most of these nesting on islets that are free from mammalian predators. Some, most notably the two species of kittiwakes (*Rissa*) from the Far North, have evolved a preference for nesting on steep cliffs. Within the marine realm, gulls display a tremendous diversity of feeding styles. Large, heavy-billed species such as the great black-backed (*Larus marinus*), glaucous (*Larus hyperboreus*), and kelp gulls frequently prey on smaller birds and mammals, while tiny species such as the little gull (*Larus minutus*), Bonaparte's gull (*Larus philadelphia*), and Ross' gull dip along the water's surface in dainty, ternlike fashion, searching for small prey items. Heermann's gulls (*Larus heermanni*) and gray gulls often probe in beach sand in the manner of a sandpiper, and a great many species scavenge along the shorelines or form flocks at concentrations of bait fish, squid, or crustaceans at the ocean's surface. Some species, such as the laughing gull (*Larus atricilla*) and Heermann's gull, closely attend diving brown pelicans (*Pelecanus occidentalis*), picking up morsels here and there that have spilled from a pelican's pouch. The unique swallow-tailed gull (*Creagrus furcatus*), breeding mainly on the Galapagos Islands, is largely nocturnal in habit, feeding on fish and squid; its large eyes hint at its preference for night life.

Terns, over forty species strong, have the appearance of slender-winged, buoyant gulls. Their slim, pointed bills are well suited to picking up fish and other prey, which they obtain by dipping to the water's surface or plunge-diving from the air. Some terns, including the widespread black tern (*Chlidonias niger*) and gull-billed tern (*Sterna nilotica*), hawk for insects over shallow water, marshes, and even open fields. But others, particularly the sooty tern (*Sterna fuscata*) and related species, the black and brown noddies (*Anous minutus* and *A. stolidus*), the diminutive blue-gray noddy (*Procelsterna cerulea*), and the ethereal white tern (*Gygis alba*), are exclusively marine in habit, wandering widely over the tropical seas. Noddies and white terns are not plungers; instead, they patter along the surface much in the manner of a storm-petrel, or swoop down to capture small fish or squid that have become airborne to escape tuna or other predatory fish; in their pursuit of the same prey, such terns and fish form a close association in the tropical oceans.

Nesting in dense colonies that may number millions of pairs, the sooty tern is one of the more abundant tropical marine species. Sooties are exceedingly buoyant and efficient fliers, winging their way around the oceans for several years before reaching breeding age, and rarely if ever alighting on the sea or coming ashore.

Unlike the gulls, the terns are most diverse in tropical and subtropical regions, but a number of species also nest at high latitudes. Among these, the arctic tern (*Sterna paradisaea*) is renowned for its long-distance migrations; departing from their far northern breeding grounds, arctic terns migrate to similar latitudes in the sub-Antarctic—a round-trip route that may exceed 20,000 miles. Only a few species, among them certain shearwaters, tundra-nesting shorebirds, and the south polar skua (*Catharacta maccormicki*), come close to rivaling the arctic tern's travels.

Skimmers—ternlike birds of coasts, lakes, and rivers—have evolved one of the most unusual foraging techniques of any bird. There are three closely related species, one each in the warmer regions of North and South America, Africa, and the Indian subcontinent. A skimmer's bill is so compressed on the sides that it appears knifelike; the lower mandible extends well beyond the upper one. Skimmers fly low over the water with the bill agape, the long lower mandible cutting the surface; when the bird encounters prey, it snaps the bill shut. Special shock-absorbing tissue in the head and neck combine with the highly adapted bill to facilitate this fishing procedure. The skimmer's needle-in-a-haystack approach to foraging requires still water and good concentration of prey; but because the method is mainly tactile, skimmers can feed easily at night, when small prey may be more abundant at the surface. Like many gulls and terns, skimmers have brightly colored bills; the color may serve a function in social and parent-chick interactions.

The gull-like jaegers (*Stercorarius*) and skuas (*Catharacta*) are powerful fliers—the smaller jaegers somewhat like falcons of the sea, and the skuas reminiscent of the heavier hawks. The jaegers and the great skua (*Catharacta skua*) breed on arctic tundra of Eurasia and North America; related skuas breed at high southerly latitudes. Some south polar skuas (well-named, as individuals have been seen virtually over the South Pole) migrate from their Antarctic breeding grounds well into the northern oceans. In summer, jaegers lead a predatory existence, feeding on lemmings and small birds and their eggs. But for the rest of the year, jaegers are aggressive oceanic pirates: adroitly pursuing terns and gulls, jaegers intimidate these birds and snatch fish or other prey from them. Skuas fill the roles of predator, pirate, and scavenger throughout the year.

From the gull and tern assemblage to the frigatebirds (*Fregata*) is a giant leap for the taxonomist, but only a small step for the ecologist. The frigatebirds, distant relatives of the pelicans, fulfill a gull-like niche in the tropical seas. The five species, distributed through most of the warmer coastal and oceanic regions, are skilled at picking fish and squid from the ocean's surface, but also scavenge at the water's surface, and prey on seabird chicks. Like the jaegers, frigatebirds also engage in kleptoparasitism—stealing prey from other birds. In their tropical haunts, the frigatebirds' chief victims are their diving cousins, the boobies.

Frigatebirds are remarkable, dynamic soarers; their very high ratio of wing surface to body weight allows them to glide effortlessly in the tropical breezes, and to cover great distances along shorelines and for some distance offshore. In courtship, male frigatebirds inflate their brilliant red, balloon-like gular pouches; these elegant soaring birds—all black, except for the bright scarlet throat pouch—are an unforgettable sight at their tropical nesting islets.

Opposite. *One of the most beautiful gulls in the world, the swallow-tailed gull (Creagrus furcatus) of the Galapagos is the most unusual. It feeds on squid and small fish that swarm at the ocean surface at night. It has a unique clicking call that scientists suggest may be a form of echo-location—an aid in finding its nest in the darkness. Its eyes are unusually large, and a large white mark on the bill must help a begging chick to feed in the dark. This gulls' nocturnal habits enable both adults to stand guard at their nest, defending it against daytime attacks by frigatebirds.* (Hans D. Dossenbach)

First, second, and third overleaves. *The ubiquitous herring gull (Larus argentatus) is known on freshwater and saltwater shores across the entire Northern Hemisphere, from the Arctic to the tropics. An omnivorous glutton, it will eat absolutely anything alive or dead, from man's garbage to the eggs of other seabirds, stuffing itself so full it cannot fly. It will catch its own fish or steal its neighbors' meal, drop shellfish from aloft until they smash on the rocks, glean crustaceans, worms, insects, mice, blueberries from tidepool, beach, field, marsh, or bog. The herring gull has a large and meaningful vocal repertoire and a long life span of up to thirty-six years, and is a long-distance traveler; first-year birds migrate nearly a thousand miles from their nest site.* (Steven C. Wilson/Entheos; Fred Bruemmer; Klas Rune/ Naturfotograferna)

Opposite. *Nesting black-legged kittiwakes* (Rissa tridactyla) *crowd the narrow ledges of a sea stack in Alaska's Kachemak Bay. The only gull that drinks salt water exclusively, and the only one that can swim underwater to feed on plankton, it is the most oceanic of all gulls and breeds in astonishing numbers on sea cliffs in northern waters around the globe. At some favored nesting cliffs, gatherings of as many as 100,000 kittiwakes, screaming their name to the arctic wind, are not unusual.* (Jeff Foott)

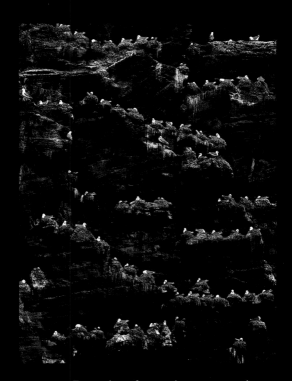

Above. *Despite the noise, a nesting colony of kittiwakes, like this one on a cliff in the Lofoten Islands of Norway, is an orderly place. The nests—deep cups of seaweed, moss, and grass plastered together with mud carried in the bill and stamped into shape with the birds' webbed feet—are carefully placed on level spots on the steep precipice, just out of reach of a pair's nearest neighbors. Streaks of white guano mark each breeding site, used year after year by veteran nesters. Kittiwakes come ashore only to propagate their kind, and spend the remainder of the year far out at sea.* (Roland Nilsson/Naturfotograferna)

Left. *As with the herring gull in North America, the population of the silver gull* (Larus novaehollandiae) *in Australia has exploded in recent years due to burgeoning refuse dumps. It is now Australia's most common seabird.* (Hans D. Dossenbach)

Above. *With raucous calls, great black-backed gulls* (Larus marinus) *celebrate a successful raid on the nests of double-crested cormorants on a rocky North Atlantic islet. This large gull is a voracious predator not only on eggs and young, but on adults of almost any seabird smaller than itself.* (John F. O'Connor, M.D./Photo/Nats)

Above and left. *A young ring-billed gull* (Larus delawarensis) *takes a vigorous bath in the receding tide off Long Island, New York. Water birds typically bathe while floating, and cleaning their feathers and skin is less important than wetting the plumage for effective preening and oiling. The ring-billed gull is widespread in North America, particularly on inland waters. They often follow tractors to pick up insects in freshly plowed fields.* (Robert Villani)

Above. *Royal terns* (Sterna maxima) *display on a beach at Padre Island in Texas. This large tern is a common sight on the southern shores of North America, where it dives for fish from heights of as much as sixty feet.* (Jon Farrar)

Opposite. *To local residents on the coast of Peru and Chile, the Inca tern* (Larosterna inca) *is* la mona, *or "the nun," because its bizarre appearance suggests a woman in religious habit and collar. Inca terns nest in cavities in guano—the only tern to nest under cover.* (Frank S. Todd)

Opposite and above. *For Forster's
tern* (Sterna forsteri) *as with many
water birds, courtship feeding is a
necessary prelude to copulation. At
Alkali Lake in the Nebraska
Sandhills, a female Forster's tern
begs like a chick from a fencepost
standing in three feet of water.
Hovering over her, the male offers
a succession of small fish—three
within a two-minute span. Mating
occurred twice during a forty-five-
minute period, the female turning
into the stiff wind so the male could
alight on her back.* (Chuck Gordon;
Jon Farrar)

Left. *Its bill open and insistently begging for food as usual, a downy young Caspian tern (Sterna caspia) stands with its parents on the sandy shore in an Audubon Society sanctuary at Aransas Bay in Texas. The largest tern in the world, the scarlet-billed Caspian often acts more like a gull than a tern, preying on the chicks and eggs of smaller seabirds and robbing other terns as they bring food to their nests nearby. The Caspian tern nests on every continent except South America and Antarctica.* (Steven C. Kaufman)

Top two rows. *Most terns lay one or two eggs in a shallow depression in the sand, and then carefully tend the chicks until they are able to fly, but noddies build nests of seaweed in bushes, and the black tern builds a floating nest in a marsh.*
From the top row at the left to the bottom row at the right, shown here are the lesser noddy (Anous tenuirostris), *the arctic* (Sterna paradisaea), *black* (Chlidonias nigra), *sooty* (Sterna fuscata), *least* (Sterna antillarum), *and elegant terns* (Sterna elegans), *all terns.* (Michael and Irene Morcombe; Alvin E. Staffan; Tim Fitzharris; Eric Hosking; Barry W. Mansell; Anthony Mercieca)

Overleaf. *"Creative license gone mad" is how one visitor to the Galapagos Islands described the courtship display of the great frigatebird* (Fregata minor). *Shriveled pink skin for most of the year, the male's gular pouch turns scarlet for three or four weeks at the beginning of the nesting season, and is blown up like a huge balloon.* (Michel Bourque/Valan Photos)

Above and opposite. *Both the eggs and chicks are perfectly camouflaged as they lie in the shallow depression in the sand the black skimmer* (Rynchops niger) *uses as a nest. The bill of an adult black skimmer, a species of North and South America, deserves close scrutiny. The bladelike lower mandible is longer than the upper, and the bird feeds by plowing the water at a rate of twenty feet per second with the mandible immersed nearly to the mouth. When the mandible strikes a surface-feeding fish, it snaps closed.* (Barry W. Mansell; Steven C. Kaufman)

Below. *The eggs of a common ringed plover* (Charadrius hiaticula) *vanish among water-worn stones on the English seashore. Shingle or sandy beaches near the high-water mark are the favored nesting sites of this mellow-voiced shorebird, well-known to European bird watchers but rarely seen in North America. Nests on sand beaches are usually camouflaged with pebbles or shell-fragments. The four eggs are laid over a six-day period; both parents incubate and tend the young, and a second clutch of eggs is often laid in the same nest.* (Brian M. Rogers/ Biofotos)

Variations on a Bill

They arrived in the night, circling down to the place where the low moon revealed the glistening of tidal flats, their haunting whistles echoing in the darkness. For several days they have stayed here, resting and feeding, their daily cycle of activity governed more by the rise and fall of the tides than by the time of day or night. But they will not stay much longer. The black-bellied plovers (*Pluvialis squatarola*) are in their most elegant plumage of the year, black and white and silvery gray, a sure sign that they are on their way to their nesting grounds far to the north. Some day soon—or some night—they will take to the air, the flock climbing higher and higher, and aiming for the northern horizon; they may fly for a thousand miles before they put down again.

The plovers, sandpipers, and related groups form the suborder Charadrii, which includes some 200 species of birds found around the world. A few of these inhabit swampy woods and a few more live on dry open plains, but the majority are birds of beaches, mudflats, marshes, or coastal rocks. Collectively they are known as "shorebirds."

In the places where water meets land, tiny creatures are often extremely common. They may be insects, mollusks, crustaceans, or any number of other animals varying in size from microscopic to several inches long. Because these creatures are diverse and abundant, the shorebirds that feed upon them are also diverse, and often abundant.

The key to variety among the shorebirds—the reason why so many different kinds can share the same habitats—is that each species has its own particular method of feeding. And the different feeding habits are reflected in the wide variety of bill shapes in this group. Shorebird bills may be short or long, stout or thin, blunt or needle-pointed or flattened at the tip; they may be upcurved or downcurved or straight, or even curved to one side. Shorebirds with very short bills, including most plovers, tend to feed on things they can see, capturing their food from the surface of the sand or mud. Shorebirds with longer bills often forage by probing in the mud, finding food by feeling for it. Of course, there are many shorebirds that do some of both, and many of the habitual probing types will pick up food from the surface if they happen to see it.

The sandpiper family (Scolopacidae) is large—nearly ninety species—and varied, with the greatest diversity of bill shapes among the shorebird clan. The variety among this family is suggested by the many different names given to its members. They are not all called sandpipers; the group also contains the curlews, godwits, snipes, turnstones, yellowlegs, dowitchers, woodcocks, tattlers, stints, knots, and phalaropes.

A dumpy sandpiper known as the long-billed dowitcher (*Limnodromus scolopaceus*) spends most of the year around freshwater ponds, where it probes in the mud for edible organisms. Searching for food, it stands in one place and methodically probes with a vertical up-and-down "sewing-machine" motion, moving on only after it has thoroughly explored one spot. Because its bill is so long, this dowitcher can take full advantage of the food available in one area. The closely related short-billed dowitcher (*Limnodromus griseus*) is usually found along the coast. The short-bill cannot probe as deeply, but because it lives in tidal areas and follows the tide in and out, it does not need to explore any one spot so thoroughly for food.

Several other sandpipers are longer-billed than the dowitchers. The impressive bill of the big marbled godwit (*Limosa fedoa*) is not only long, but also slightly upcurved; it is used for probing in the mud. The even longer bill of the long-billed curlew (*Numenius americanus*) curves down instead. Both of these big cinnamon-colored shorebirds nest in prairie regions of the American West, but spend the winter on coastal mudflats; their bills are apparently well adapted to feeding in both habitats.

But sandpipers do not have to be so large, nor so long-billed, to use the probing method of feeding. The dunlin (*Calidris alpina*) and the western sandpiper (*Calidris mauri*), for example, are hardly larger than sparrows, with bills less than two inches long; but they can be seen probing away on the mudflats during their migrations, often in flocks by the hundreds. They find their food just below the surface, probably taking items that would be too small to interest a curlew or a godwit.

A different method of foraging has been perfected by the ruddy turnstone (*Arenaria interpres*). Its short bill is rather thick at the base and pointed at the tip, forming a narrow wedge. This shape is ideal for the bird's habit of inserting its bill under small rocks and flipping them over to see what lurks beneath—turning stones, true to its name.

The three sandpipers known as phalaropes are unique among shorebirds in that they do much of their foraging as they swim. Floating lightly on the water, phalaropes use their long, thin bills to pick at insect larvae, tiny crustaceans, and other creatures on or just below the surface. Often the phalaropes spin in circles, an action that may stir up the water and bring small organisms up to where they can be seen.

In a separate family are the avocets and stilts, large shorebirds with elegant patterns and graceful movements. The American avocet (*Recurvirostra americana*) has a narrow bill that is distinctly upcurved at the tip. Immersing the bill tip in the water while wading in the shallows, the avocet sweeps it from side to side with rapid "nibbling" movements, capturing insect larvae just above the muddy bottom of the pond. Its relative the black-necked stilt (*Himantopus mexicanus*) has a bill that looks almost needle-thin and needle-straight; the stilt tends to pick at creatures on the surface of the water.

Also in their own family are the several kinds of oystercatchers, big stocky shorebirds found around the coastlines of the world. Some oystercatchers are sooty black all over, while others are patterned in black and white, but all have long, thick, bright red bills that they use in foraging for mollusks. "Oystercatching" is a slightly misleading term. Actually, the bird generally discovers its prey by surprise: finding a bivalve with its shell slightly open, the oystercatcher uses a quick jab of its bill to immobilize the creature within, and then pries the shell open to extract its meal.

After the sandpipers, the plovers form the second-largest family of shorebirds, with more than sixty species worldwide. Most plovers have short bills, which are of limited use for probing in the mud; these birds tend to employ a visual approach, running about with abrupt starts and stops, grabbing small insects and other creatures. Because they do not need to forage in wet mud, plovers are often seen on rather dry sandy beaches, and some kinds habitually live on dry grasslands and fields far from the water.

A typical small plover of the mudflats is the semipalmated plover (*Charadrius semipalmatus*). Often it forages on very wet mud, but when it is seeking food on drier sand, it will sometimes quiver one foot over the surface of the sand, perhaps startling tiny creatures into moving and thereby revealing their location.

One of the oddest bill shapes among shorebirds is displayed by a small New Zealand plover called the wrybill (*Anarynchus frontalis*). At first glance, seen from the side, the bird's bill does not seem unusual; but viewed head-on, or from above, the tip of the bill can be seen to curve sharply to the right. The wrybill uses this odd instrument to probe under small stones in shallow water, and it sometimes performs a sideways sweeping motion through the mud with its bill.

The greatest shorebird nursery is the vast tundra region, north of treeline, that stretches across the arctic slopes of North America, Europe, and Asia. This huge area, encompassing many hundreds of thousands of square miles, teems with life during the brief arctic summer. Spurred by a full twenty-four hours of daylight, the low-growing tundra plants burst into bloom, and billions of insects and other tiny organisms must complete their life cycles before the next long winter.

The tundra also teems with shorebirds in summer: there are many areas of the Far North where a dozen or more species nest. They wear their most striking patterns of the year at this season, and many sing and perform flight displays to advertise their claims to their nesting territories. Whereas songbirds in the temperate zone often proclaim their territorial limits by singing from the treetops, the shorebirds on the tundra—lacking treetops from which to sing—often take to the air; many species perform elaborate displays in which they fly with exaggeratedly slow wingbeats, or with the wings fluttered stiffly below the horizontal, while they utter loud, musical whistles or trills. The songs of the shorebirds are the most characteristic sounds of the tundra in summer.

But for the greater part of the year, when the land is locked in ice and covered with snow, the tundra is no place for a shorebird. Most shorebirds stay on their arctic nesting grounds for a surprisingly short time: they may not arrive until early June, and if their attempt at nesting should fail, they may be southbound again by the beginning of July. Even those that nest successfully and raise young may be on the tundra for no more than two months. Then they spend the rest of the year on the world's beaches and muddy shores.

A good example is provided by the sanderling (*Calidris alba*), the pale sandpiper that is typically seen running up the beach ahead of each advancing wave, and then turning to run back down the beach after the receding water. Sanderlings nest almost entirely north of the Arctic Circle, but in winter they are found on beaches south to the southern tip of South America, southern Africa, India, Australia, New Zealand, and many oceanic islands. The whimbrel (*Numenius phaeopus*), ruddy turnstone, and black-bellied plover also have nonbreeding ranges that are nearly as global as that of the sanderling.

In commuting between the south temperate latitudes and the northern tundra, shorebirds must undertake great journeys; some individuals make round trips of 10,000 miles each year. Often they make these migrations in leaps of many hundreds of miles at a time, and they must feed heavily for several days to build up reserves for such a flight. There are a few favored places where food is temporarily abundant and where huge numbers of shorebirds pause annually in their migration. One such area is Delaware Bay, in New Jersey and Delaware, where the horseshoe crabs (*Limulus polyphemus*) come ashore to lay billions of eggs in late May. Unbelievable hordes of shorebirds swarm on these flats during this brief period; there may be more than half a million shorebirds on these shores at one time. And then suddenly they are gone, continuing on their tremendous journey, vanishing over the horizon.

Opposite. *A pair of large, bright yellow facial wattles that drape below the bill give the masked lapwing* (Vanellus miles) *of Australia a distinctive if bizarre appearance. Masked lapwings are familiar birds along lakes and rivers, on tidal flats, and especially on grazed pastures—their preferred nesting sites. Young birds remain with their parents for eight months, and flocks of several hundred masked lapwings assemble during the nonbreeding period, scouring grasslands for worms, insects, and seeds during cold weather.* (Jean-Paul Ferrero/Auscape International)

First overleaf. *It is high tide at Gray's Harbor, a critical refueling stop on the Washington coast for shorebirds migrating to Alaska nesting grounds. The warm light of early morning highlights the rusty underparts of a resting long-billed dowitcher* (Limnodromus scolopaceus) *while dunlins* (Calidris alpina) *doze in the background. The long-billed dowitcher is bound for the soggy tundra of the northern Alaska coast. Four eggs will be laid in a damp, moss-lined nest. During early incubation, the male dowitcher stands guard against intruders, then relieves his mate for the hatching and rearing of the young.* (Tom and Pat Leeson)

Second overleaf. *Ruddy turnstones* (Arenaria interpres), *pausing on their flight to Canada's high Arctic islands while awaiting spring's advance, crowd a rock in a shallow pool near Hudson Bay. This plump, strikingly marked shorebird is named for its habit of flipping aside small stones with its bill to nab hiding invertebrates. In hot pursuit of a burrowing crab, a turnstone will dig a hole larger than itself in the sand. Ruddy turnstones nest around the North Pole, arriving on their breeding grounds in late May or early June as the snow melts from the tundra. Both sexes incubate the four eggs, but the female departs long before the young birds have fledged.* (Wayne Lankinen)

Opposite. *An immature semipalmated plover* (Charadrius semipalmatus), *southbound in August from its birthplace on a gravelly river bar in Alaska, searches the stony shore of Puget Sound for mollusks and crustaceans. One of the more abundant North American shorebirds, the semipalmated plover is found throughout the continent during migration, and winters from the southern shores of the United States to Argentina and Chile.* (Tim Fitzharris)

Above. *Tidal flats along the Pacific Coast from California to Peru are the winter quarters for uncountable numbers of western sandpipers* (Calidris mauri). *Here they probe the mud for small invertebrates, but on their breeding grounds along the Alaska coast, western sandpipers feed almost exclusively on abundant insect life. Both male and female return to the nesting territory occupied the previous spring.* (Tim Fitzharris)

Above. *Taking a relaxing stretch after a long migration from the Arctic, a juvenile red-necked phalarope* (Phalaropus lobatus) *floats on a pond at a wildlife refuge near New York City's Kennedy Airport. A buoyant swimmer with lobed toes, this seagoing sandpiper spins in a tight circle, stirring up miniscule animal prey.* (Arthur Morris)

Left. *A familiar shorebird in winter on both coasts of North America, a black-bellied plover* (Pluvialis squatarola) *ruffles its feathers in the chill wind. Its plaintive three-note flight call is one of the most memorable sounds of beach and estuary.* (Arthur Morris)

181

Right. *The handsome American avocet (Recurvirostra americana) feeds like a spoonbill, sweeping its sharply upcurved bill from side to side through the muddy water, picking up aquatic insects, shrimp, and floating seeds.* (G.C. Kelley)

Top two rows. *It is possible to see all of these shorebirds at once, feeding on a wave-washed beach. Variations in bill shape are what enable so many species of shorebirds to feed together without overtaxing the food supply. Each species has a bill that enables it to seek out a different prey, to probe for its food at a different depth, or to forage in a slightly different way. All of these species are feeding on the beach, in sand that is still wet from receding waves. Bills that are upcurved, downcurved, long and needle-like, or short and slender, all are special food-capturing equipment for the species that possesses them.*

From the top row at the left to the bottom row at the right, the species are a marbled godwit (Limosa fedoa), *a young black-necked stilt* (Himantopus mexicanus), *a sanderling* (Calidris alba), *a long-billed curlew* (Numenius americanus), *a willet* (Catoptrophorus semipalmatus), *and a whimbrel* (Numenius phaeopus), *actually a curlew that also feeds on berries on grassy slopes that face the sea.* (Jeff Foott; Arthur Morris; Lynn M. Stone; Jon Farrar; Ben Goldstein/Root Resources; Irene Hinke Sacilotto)

Above, opposite, and overleaf. *The funereal plumage of the black oystercatcher* (Haematopus bachmani) *is a perfect match for its haunts—the rocky Pacific shore from the Aleutian Islands to Baja California.*

The oystercatcher's knifelike, chisel-tipped bill is designed for preying on mussels, chitons, and limpets that cling to wave-washed rocks and tidal shoals. Mussels that are still open at ebbtide are paralyzed with a stab deep into the shell, and the bill is deftly used as a lever to dislodge limpets. The black oystercatcher nests atop rocks and pinnacles; a month after hatching, the two or three chicks are able to prey on shellfish. (Jeff Foott; overleaf, Steven C. Wilson/ Entheos)

Below. *The gray-headed albatross* (Diomedea chrysostoma) *glides over the southern oceans around the pole, nesting on sub-Antarctic islands and following the Humboldt current as far north as Peru. Sailors of another day believed that albatrosses brought stormy weather; the superstition has an element of truth, for these ship-followers ride the wild winds with few wingbeats. Fearless of man on their nesting colonies, which were once ravaged for the feather trade, they were called "mollymawks," from a Dutch phrase meaning "stupid gull." Japanese fishermen called them "fool birds."* (Graham Robertson/ Auscape International)

Navigating the
High Seas

Cotton fluffs of tradewind clouds dot the tropical skyscape; below, the ocean rolls away endlessly to all horizons. The warm winds stir up a light chop on the water's surface; the liquid murmur of the water, cut by the bow of our ketch, softly breaks the silence. We are a thousand miles away from any land in the eastern tropical Pacific Ocean, well away from the domain of all but a handful of the world's 9,100 species of birds. The sight of any bird might seem incongruous in this vast medium of sky and sea. And yet ahead, with an arcing glide, a long-winged bird cuts above the horizon, only to disappear again behind a swell, then glide into view once more. After a minute or two it is gone, vanished into the vast interface of ocean and sky.

Then more appear. Gleaming white below, gray marked with black and white above, they swing close by our stern, deviating slightly from their purposeful journey. Their stout black bills, hooked strongly at the tip, show the odd, tubular external nostrils characteristic of only one group of birds—the "tubenoses" of the order Procellariiformes, which includes the albatrosses, petrels, and their kin. The birds we have seen are white-necked petrels (*Pterodroma externa*), belonging to a genus of perhaps the most highly oceanic of all birds, the gadfly petrels.

Smaller petrels speed by, moving in faster, tighter arcs over the surface; these are black-winged petrels (*Pterodroma nigripennis*). Occasionally we encounter a bird on the water, riding high and buoyant, but escaping into the currents of air at our approach. Then an even smaller and very different seabird bounds out of the trough of a swell and into view. It hardly seems to fly, but rather hang-glides just over the surface, pushed along in zigs and zags by paddling motions of its feet. It wheels quickly around to pick up a morsel off the water, then hops erratically off into the swells. This bird is a white-throated storm-petrel (*Nesofregetta fuliginosa*), the largest of the storm-petrels (Hydrobatidae), a group containing species as small as a swallow. There is indeed bird life at these great distances from land, and while we might encounter certain pelagic terns, and perhaps the occasional passing booby, frigatebird, or tropicbird, it is the tubenoses that are most at home here.

On a fishing vessel well off New England, bumping around in green, choppy seas and surrounded by a frenzy of bird life, one sees the usual flock of gulls wheeling around the boat, keenly interested in scraps and unwanted sandwiches. And gannets flap by from time to time. But two species are particularly numerous. One is a slender-winged, gull-like bird, flying rapidly with stiff wingbeats and smooth glides. Gray-brown above, white below, white-rumped and black-capped, it is the greater shearwater (*Puffinus gravis*), and by its tubular external nostrils we can tell that this is a relative of the birds we met in the tropics. Hundreds of these shearwaters stream past, and now and then a flock feeds busily upon fish at the water's surface. Another bird appears; just seven inches long, it sometimes seems more like butterfly than bird, tap-dancing on air just above the water's surface. This is another storm-petrel, the Wilson's (*Oceanites oceanicus*), and we encounter it by the thousands as we cut through the North Atlantic summer.

The greater shearwaters and Wilson's storm-petrels that are seen in such abundance are not residents of the North Atlantic. The world's three million pairs of greater shearwaters nest mainly on the islands of the Tristan da Cunha group, in the South Atlantic. Some experts estimate that Wilson's storm-petrel may number 100 million; the species' breeding colonies ring the Antarctic continent. It is not just the abundance of many tubenose species that is astounding, but also the magnitude and geographical scale of the birds' migratory movements. Along the California coast on a good May day, an observer might count as many as half a million sooty shearwaters (*Puffinus griseus*) streaming northward; that observer would be hard-pressed to find a more abundant bird species in that region. Yet these shearwaters have come to California from breeding colonies off Chile, Australia, and New Zealand. And in the Bering Sea, one of the most abundant in the summer months is the short-tailed shearwater (*Puffinus tenuirostris*), a species breeding only off southeastern Australia!

The tube-nosed seabirds are most diverse in the wind-blown sub-Antarctic seas, with their towering swells of cold water. This is a highly productive region, supporting teeming populations of seabirds. Here, as we approach the tip of the Antarctic Peninsula, we find the largest of the tubenoses, the wandering albatross (*Diomedea exulans*), soaring on wings that span eleven feet. There are other, smaller albatrosses here too: the black-browed (*Diomedea melanophris*) and the light-mantled sooty (*Phoebetria palpebrata*), as well as the similar-sized southern giant petrel (*Macronectes giganteus*). Antarctic fulmars (*Fulmarus glacialoides*) and the ubiquitous, pied Cape petrels (*Daption capense*) wheel about behind the visitor's boat, and pure white snow petrels (*Pagodroma nivea*) gleam in the low sun against the dark water, as if born of icebergs. Prions, or "whalebirds" (*Pachtyptila*), plough the surface, straining crustaceans with their specialized bills. And our friends from the North Atlantic, the Wilson's storm-petrels, are abundant here, close to their natal islets, in the Antarctic summer. The ordinal name Procellariiformes comes from the Latin word *procella*, meaning "storm"; and indeed the tubenoses are most at home in these stormy southern seas.

The tube-nosed birds include the largest and smallest of the seabirds, some of the most abundant and some of the most threatened birds in the world. Among them are birds of high and of equatorial latitudes, of the coldest and the warmest ocean waters. Some ninety-five species strong, they are ocean birds *par excellence*, mysterious and endlessly fascinating.

Procellariiform birds all share the feature of tubular external nostrils, but they have other traits in common as well. All are densely feathered and have a distinctive, musty odor. Their three front toes are fully webbed, and the hind toe is reduced or absent. All have bills that are strongly hooked at the tip. Being exclusively marine, they possess several attributes that allow them to cope with a saltwater existence—most notably the large and efficient nasal salt glands, which act like tiny desalination plants, extracting salt from sea water. Many tubenoses demonstrate a well-developed olfactory sense.

Taxonomists divide the tubenoses into four families: the albatrosses (Diomedeidae), the petrels and shearwaters (Procellariidae), the storm-petrels (Hydrobatidae), and the diving-petrels (Pelecanoididae). The group as a whole is highly diverse; its members range in size from the tiny storm-petrels to the huge wandering albatross. But the diversity of tubenoses is perhaps best expressed by wing shape, and in particular by two ratios that dictate flight performance and which reflect the different life-styles of these species.

One such ratio is called wing-loading, which expresses the amount of body weight supported by the surface area of the wings. The lightweight storm-petrels, with relatively long, broad wings, have low wing-loading. They fly buoyantly, low over the water, and cover considerable distances as they seek food particles at the surface. Storm-petrels do not dive. At the other extreme are the diving petrels, heavy-bodied birds with small, pointed wings and high wing-loading. Ecologically and structurally, they are strikingly similar to the auklets of the Northern Hemisphere, whom we met in a previous chapter. As the name suggests, diving-petrels are expert divers; they use their reduced wings for underwater propulsion and whirring flight through the air. The most highly wing-loaded of the seabirds are the penguins, which are flightless; most ornithologists agree that the penguins and the tubenoses are one another's closest relatives.

Even within the group that includes the petrels and the shearwaters, there is variation in wing-loading that corresponds closely to feeding habits. These shearwaters with longer, broader wings pursue prey at the water's surface; examples are Cory's shearwater (*Calonectris diomedea*) of the Atlantic and Buller's shearwater (*Puffinus bulleri*) of the Pacific. Other shearwaters, such as the sooty and the Manx (*Puffinus puffinus*), both with relatively high wing-loading, often dive for food. All shearwaters are powerful flyers, however, covering enormous expanses of ocean in their wanderings.

The other important ratio is the aspect ratio, which is essentially a comparison of wing length to wing area. The highest aspect ratios in birds occur in certain large albatrosses that have exceptionally long and narrow wings. This structure is an adaptation for dynamic soaring, an energetically inexpensive way to cover tremendous distances by exploiting wind currents over the water's surface. Rounded-winged storm-petrels, such as the Wilson's, show a relatively low aspect ratio; what they lack in dynamic soaring ability, they make up for in maneuverability, showing adeptness at rapidly picking food particles off the surface of the sea.

Though the tubenoses are more completely wed to the sea than any other group of birds, they still must come ashore to coastal or oceanic islands to nest. The largest tubenoses build nests of vegetation directly on the ground, but most other species burrow or nest in sheltered sites among rocks or vegetation. Nesting is a drawn-out affair, and the reproductive rate is low: one egg per year (or even every other year in the large albatrosses); furthermore, some of the larger species do not even reach breeding age until they are five to ten years old. This low breeding rate has accelerated the suffering of many populations at the hands of man. In particular, predators such as cats and rats introduced to otherwise "safe" nesting islands have taken a toll on many species.

It is a source of wonder that birds such as petrels or shearwaters can fledge from a tiny spot of land on the vast oceans, wander these oceans to feed and to mature over the next several years, and then successfully navigate back to their natal island to breed. One must consider, however, that the ocean is not as uniform an environment as it might appear to our land-based sensibilities. Most tubenoses feed within preferred ranges of sea surface temperature and salinity, and the birds are probably very sensitive to currents, convergences, wind patterns, and other environmental variables. Celestial, magnetic, and even olfactory cues could certainly play a role in tubenose navigation.

Sailors have used the sun's position, the pattern of the stars, and magnetic compasses to navigate the seas for many centuries. The Procellariiformes, which have wandered the oceans far longer than sea-faring man, almost certainly use similar cues, but integrate them into a deep, thorough, multi-sensory perception of the marine environment.

Opposite and overleaf. *Abundant and wide-ranging, the black-browed albatross* (Diomedea melanophris) *is a circumpolar bird of southern latitudes that wanders regularly into the North Atlantic, although it never occurs in the North Pacific. In one famous occurrence, a black-browed albatross lived and migrated with nesting gannets on the Faroe Islands, between Iceland and Britain, for thirty-four years until it was shot by a misguided hunter. But for most albatrosses, the windless doldrums at the equator have proved to be an impenetrable barrier.* (François Gohier)

Left. *A characteristic display posture of the world's largest and most famous albatross is one in which the bill is pointed skyward and the wings are held out, often for long periods. The wandering albatross (Diomedea exulans) has the greatest wingspan of any bird—nearly twelve feet. One of these birds can live as long as seventy or eighty years, and can do a lot of traveling in that time. A bird banded on the island of South Georgia appeared six months later off the east coast of Australia, after journeying a minimum of 13,000 miles.* (François Gohier)

Top two rows. *Courtship among the albatrosses is an elaborate, stylized affair, with much bowing, preening, scraping of bills, and groaning. All of this leads to mating, but these ceremonies also maintain the bond between the members of a pair, and can be seen all through the nesting season. A pair of black-browed albatrosses, top row, is courting at their colony at the Falkland Islands in the South Atlantic. The waved albatross (Diomedia irrorata), bottom row, the only equatorial albatross, nests in the Galapapos Islands.* (Top row, François Gohier; bottom row, Dale and Marian Zimmerman/ VIREO)

Overleaf. *The nest of a black-browed albatross is a low pillar of vegetation where male and female share incubation duties for five weeks. The parents guard the chick day and night for several more weeks until the young albatross is large enough to defend itself. An immature black-browed albatross makes its first flight when it is less than four months of age; the larger wandering albatross chick does not take wing until it is nearly ten months old.* (François Gohier)

Below. *A pair of red-throated loons (Gavia stellata) guard their newly hatched chick on a tundra pond in northern Sweden. The most widely distributed member of its family, the red-throated nests on Arctic and sub-Arctic seacoasts, lakes, and marshes around the pole, wintering as far south as China, the Mediterranean Sea, Florida, and California. But the handsome breeding plumage—highlighted by the rich chestnut throat patch that gives this loon its name—is generally seen only by visitors to the Far North. The molt from dull gray-brown winter plumage occurs after most birds have left on their spring migration.* (Janos Jurka/ Naturfotograferna)

Agile Divers

A baby horned grebe (*Podiceps auritus*), hatching out of the egg, has its first view of the world from a nest that bobs up and down with each passing ripple. The nest is a floating mass of plant material, anchored to a reed in the shallows, with water all around. If the young grebe moves a few inches in any direction it will fall into the water. But that is not a problem: a few hours after hatching, the grebe chick is ready to swim, ready to embark upon a life of being comfortable in and under the water.

A baby red-throated loon (*Gavia stellata*) begins life in a nest near a lake on the northern tundra; it may stay in the nest for about a day before it takes to the water. Within a few weeks, both the loon and the grebe will be superb swimmers, expert at diving and at swimming beneath the surface.

Are the loon and grebe families closely related to each other? For many years they were thought to be, because they have many things in common. These are birds that make their living by swimming underwater. Their food consists mainly of small fish, as well as aquatic insects, crustaceans, and other arthropods. Loons and grebes dive from the surface, often leaping in with their heads arched forward and downward; like good submarines, however, they can also alter their buoyancy so that they sink slowly beneath the surface with no obvious effort. Sometimes their wings are held partway open underwater, and pumped for additional steering or speed, but more typically their wings are folded tightly against their bodies during a dive. They propel themselves through the depths mainly by paddling with their large feet.

For maximum efficiency in pushing them through the water, the legs of loons and grebes are positioned very far back on their bodies. This design makes them awkward on land, where they generally have to push themselves along on their bellies. And in order to take flight, they have to run along the surface of the water, with much splashing and furious flapping of wings, before they become airborne; most are unable to take off from land. Occasionally at night, a loon or grebe lands on a rain-soaked stretch of pavement, evidently mistaking the reflection for open water; the bird will be stranded there unless it is rescued.

The sexes are always alike in appearance, but all loons and most grebes go through two distinct plumages per year, changing from a brightly patterned breeding plumage into a duller winter plumage. Although most loons and many grebes spend the winter on salt water, all of them nest at freshwater lakes or ponds. A charming habit shared by loons and grebes is their practice of carrying their young: the baby birds learn to climb onto their parents' backs and ride there, sometimes staying put while the adults dive underwater.

Since these two families have so many features and habits in common, it is no wonder that they were once thought to be close relatives. Recently, more sophisticated studies have suggested that they are not at all closely related. Instead, their similarities have evolved independently, in a long and gradual process, as the birds developed adaptations to fill the same kind of niche. This phenomenon—known as "convergence"—happens because, over the eons, evolution has chanced upon the same winning combinations many separate times. Throughout the bird world, there are examples of unrelated species that have developed the same traits as they adapted to similar habitats or food sources.

There are five kinds of loons (called "divers" in Great Britain), all medium-sized to large swimming birds that nest in northern regions around the globe. The most familiar of them, the common loon (*Gavia immer*), spends its summers on lakes in the coniferous forest, so its summer range extends south of the Canadian border into Minnesota (where it is the official state bird), New England, and some other areas. But the other loons nest on the tundra, north of treeline, some traveling to areas well north of the Arctic Circle for the summer. Of course, most loons have to undertake major migrations to reach waters that will remain open all winter, and at some coastal points, particularly on the Pacific, it is possible to see impressive flights of southbound loons in the fall. But all of them stop before they reach tropical waters.

The twenty or so species of grebes form a more varied group, with some as large as the smallest loons and others practically as small as robins. They are found on freshwater lakes throughout the world. Those that nest the farthest north—for example, the horned grebe and the red-necked grebe (*Podiceps grisegena*), which reach the edge of arctic lands in both Eurasia and North America—have to migrate south with the arrival of cold weather, and they often spend the winter on coastal bays a thousand miles from their breeding grounds. In tropical areas, by contrast, grebes may have no need for anything more than limited local movements. Carrying this to an extreme are two species of grebes that spend their entire lives on large permanent lakes, and have actually lost the ability to fly; the short-winged grebe (*Rollandia micropterum*) is confined to Lake Titicaca and Lake Poopó, Bolivia, while the Atitlan grebe (*Podilymbus gigas*) is found only at Lake Atitlan, in Guatemala.

The characteristic voice of northern lakes in summer is the wild, weird yodelling of the common loon. At the season when it sings, the common loon is in its elegant breeding plumage, with glossy black head, white necklace, and a checkerboard pattern of black and white on the back. All of the other loons also give loud yodelling, whistling, or wailing calls in summer, and they all wear summer plumages that are crisply patterned in black, gray, and white; the small red-throated loon is further adorned with a patch of deep red on the throat. The summer finery of the loons is a far cry from their simple winter plumages, in which all are brownish-gray above and white below.

Most loons seem to mate for life, so they are often already in pairs when they arrive at their nesting areas in spring. Their courtship ceremonies are brief and simple; the birds devote more energy to defending their chosen territories against other loons. Their far-carrying voices, heard both day and night, advertise their claims, and the birds also have ritualized displays, which they use to threaten and drive away other loons that happen to land on their waters.

Because they are clumsy on land, loons usually build their nests very close to the water, so they do not have to flop along on their bellies any farther than necessary. Not that nest-building takes much effort: the nest itself is a simple mound of vegetation, sometimes only a scrape in the ground. Usually two eggs are laid, olive-brown with darker spots; they are incubated by both parents for nearly a month before they hatch.

Especially in tundra regions of the Arctic, the lake chosen as a nesting site by a pair of loons may not provide enough food for the entire family. In these cases, the parent birds may fly several miles to other lakes, or to the ocean, to bring back food for their offspring. They continue to feed their young for weeks. It takes at least six weeks before the young of the small red-throated loon are able to fly; in the larger common loon and the yellow-billed loon (*Gavia adamsii*), the young may not be capable of flight until they are ten or eleven weeks old, and they are attended by the adults the whole time. Some young loons even make their first southward migration in the close company of their parents.

For certain grebes, such as the western grebe (*Aechmophorus occidentalis*), the transition from winter plumage to breeding plumage produces only a slightly crisper pattern. But other grebes develop bright patterns and sometimes plumes, crests, or ruffs of feathers. The horned grebe, for example, which is plain gray and white in winter, takes on a summer outfit of black and rufous, with bright golden tufts or "horns" on its head. The great crested grebe (*Podiceps cristatus*) is crested all year, but in the breeding season it also wears a fanlike ruff of chestnut-and-black feathers on each side of its neck.

203

Courtship seems to be a more serious matter for grebes than for loons. Most kinds have a variety of rituals used in forming pairs, or in strengthening the pair bond. In some species, the male and female grebe will sit on the water almost within touching distance and pivot their whole bodies so that they first face toward each other, then away from each other, sometimes going on for minutes at a time. Many species have variations on a display in which members of a pair will rear up almost vertically and tread water in this position, often wagging their heads back and forth. A more elaborate version in many grebes is the "weed ceremony," in which each bird dives to pick up a mouthful of underwater weeds; they then face each other in an upright position, holding their weeds and shaking their heads in unison.

A display that is remarkable and attention-getting—especially when performed by one of the bigger grebes—involves a "race" across the water. In this ritual, as demonstrated by the western grebe, two birds begin by swimming toward each other, alternately pointing their bills at each other and dipping them in the water. When they are perhaps a foot apart, the birds suddenly turn at right angles to face the same direction, rear up out of the water, arch their necks, and speed away across the water together, paddling furiously with their feet. After racing for up to fifty yards or more, the birds dive underwater. This bizarre behavior is not solely a courtship display; it is sometimes performed by two birds that are not members of a pair, and it can involve more than two birds (sometimes as many as six).

Awkwardness on land makes nesting time as much of a challenge for the grebes as it is for the loons. Grebes solve the problem by constructing their nests *in* the water, building up from the bottom in the shallows, or anchoring floating masses of vegetation to reeds. Thus a grebe on its nest is never more than a few inches from the safety of the water.

Unlike loons, in which each pair hotly defends its own territory against intrusion by other loons, grebes often nest in loose colonies. Their nests may be packed in only a few feet apart, so long as each grebe sitting on its nest is not within jabbing distance of its neighbors. A bird nesting near the center of a dense colony may travel between open water and its nest by swimming beneath the surface, rather than risk passing too close to other pairs. The colonial nesting arrangement works well, because a large lake with food enough for many pairs of grebes may have only a few limited clumps of good nesting sites.

Grebes usually lay more eggs than loons, typically three or four, sometimes six or more. The parents will feed their young for several weeks; but unlike loons, the adult grebes almost never fly to other lakes to find food for the young. Relative flying abilities may have something to do with this. Both loons and grebes have to work hard at taking off; but although loons fly strongly once they are airborne, flight always appears to be a struggle for most grebes.

Opposite. *Golden ear tufts adorn the nuptial plumage in both sexes of the horned grebe* (Podiceps auritus). *Like the red-throated loon, this grebe is a circumpolar species; it is known as the "Slavonian grebe" in the Old World. A bird of freshwater northern marshes, it nests in loose colonies of perhaps a half-dozen pairs, anchoring a floating platform—a mass of mud and rotting vegetation—to emergent plants. Horned grebes feed on small fish and other aquatic life; when the four eggs hatch, the parents carry the downy chicks about on their backs, and even dive after food with the young aboard. In winter, minus their striking "horns," these grebes ride the ocean waves, rarely taking to the air.* (G.C. Kelley)

Opposite and above. *The western grebe* (Aechmophorus occidentalis) *is famous for its spectacular courtship display, climaxed by the partners dashing across the water on their toes, swanlike necks extended, leaving a fishtail of spray in their wake. This is a bird of western North America, nesting from the northern prairies to California in colonies that may include hundreds of pairs. The male gathers nesting material and his mate assembles it into a large platform in the bulrushes. Incubation begins when the first of three or four eggs is laid; the chicks hatch on successive days.* (Peter M. Roberts; Chuck Gordon)

Top and opposite. *Well-known to bird watchers in both North America and Europe, the common loon (Gavia immer) is a handsome bird in breeding plumage, its feathers marked with black and white. It is partial to deep-water lakes where it can dive in pursuit of its prey. This species requires seclusion, and it has been driven from many of its traditional nesting lakes by development and acid rain.* (Peter M. Roberts; Tom W. Parkin/Valan Photos)

Above. *The great crested grebe (Podiceps cristatus) of Eurasia has long black horns and a ruff of rust and black feathers that can be erected like a collar during aggressive displays.* (Manfred Wiechmann)

Overleaf. *Grebes have short wings and almost nonexistent tails; once they manage to become airborne— which they do reluctantly and with great effort—they are weak fliers, steering aloft with their feet. When threatened, they prefer to vanish underwater. The red-necked grebe (Podiceps grisegena) is found across the Northern Hemisphere, nesting on small openings in large marshes.* (Douglas Leighton)

Below. *Nearly twice the size of its commonplace relatives in North America and Europe, the giant coot* (Fulica gigantea) *is found on lakes high in the Andes of Peru, Bolivia, and northern Chile. Twenty-six inches long, and the only coot with red legs and feet, it builds a large floating nest of aquatic plants, strong enough to support a person. A platform reused and added to over several years may be ten feet in diameter. Another unusual coot of high Andean lakes is the horned coot* (Fulica cornuta); *its nest sits atop a foundation of stones the size of small potatoes, which the bird carries from shore in its beak.* (Guenter Ziesler)

Stalkers in Dense Marshes

Not all watery habitats are open. Around the world, certain types of shallow waters are filled with grasses, reeds, and other aquatic plants, forming dense marshes. And the birds that live within these marshes are not always so conspicuous.

No group of birds is more typical of marshy places the world over than the Rallidae, the rail family. By visiting a large marsh practically anywhere in North America, at dawn in spring or summer, we can encounter rails—if we listen carefully. A nasal descending laughter and a syncopated clacking sound are calls of the Virginia rail (*Rallus limicola*), while more musical whistles and whinnies announce the presence of a small rail called the sora (*Porzana carolina*). Depending on where on the North American continent we are, we may hear the grunting notes of the king rail (*Rallus elegans*), the clatter of the clapper rail (*Rallus longirostris*), the growls and chirps of the black rail (*Laterallus jamaicensis*), or the metallic ticking of the rare yellow rail (*Coturnicops noveboracensis*). There are places where three, four, even five kinds of rails may be audible from one spot.

But we could spend the rest of the day at that spot without actually seeing a single rail, because these birds are remarkably adept at staying out of sight in the dense cover of the marsh. If we wade through the marsh looking for the calling birds, one of them may eventually flush ahead of us. The rail rises clumsily from almost underfoot, beating rapidly and stiffly with short, rounded wings, its legs and long-toed feet dangling below the bird in flight. After fluttering along weakly for a dozen yards or so, it drops back into the marsh. And if we try to flush it again, we may fail to find it at all, because the rail has probably slipped away after landing.

With habits such as these, it is no wonder that rails often escape notice even in areas where they are numerous. The sora is common over most of North America, and though it is not nearly as furtive as some of its cousins, it still generally goes unseen. Like most rails, the sora is built for marshy surroundings. Its large feet and rather long toes help to keep it from sinking in soft mud. Seen from the side, the bird looks heavy and rotund, but its body is actually compressed laterally —from side to side—so that when it is seen from the front or the back it looks quite slender, thin enough to slip easily among the marsh grasses. Indeed, the expression "thin as a rail" could well apply to the sora.

Like most rails, the sora can swim—a useful skill for a bird living in such watery surroundings—but it seems to do so mainly as a way of getting across short stretches of open water, not as a regular habit. The sora's nest is a cup of grasses, hidden in the marsh, where it lays up to a dozen or more eggs, camouflaged in spotted brown. When the young hatch, they are covered with fluffy black down; they soon leave the nest to roam about in the marsh with their parents.

Not all rails are marsh birds. This is especially true in tropical areas, where habitats are most complicated. Tropical forests are often very wet places, with numerous streams and swampy spots, and some are seasonally flooded; when a rail goes walking through a rain forest, it would be hard to say at what point it ceases to be a water bird! The wood-rails (*Aramides*) of South America often wander well away from water, and the forest rails (*Rallina*) of New Guinea may be found in relatively dry jungle and scrubby forest. But even in temperate regions, the distinction between marshes and damp fields may not be clear-cut. A European rail called the corn crake (*Crex crex*) often lives in dry hayfields and pastures.

At the other extreme, some members of the rail family have taken to the water like ducks. One well-known example is the American coot (*Fulica americana*). This charcoal-colored bird swims and dives freely in the open water, and often associates with flocks of waterfowl; many people who know the coot by name assume that it is some sort of duck. But it has an un-ducklike bill, thick and chalky-white, and it pumps its head back and forth rhythmically as it swims.

Although they are omnivorous—like most members of their family—American coots tend to specialize on plant material far more than most other rails. But they have many different strategies for getting their food. Coots up-end in shallow water, and they dive and swim underwater, paddling with their feet, to bring up submerged weeds. They will also leap partway out of the water to pick leaves or insects from overhanging branches. Coots frequently steal choice items from ducks, or from each other, and for some very aggressive individuals this theft becomes a major source of food. In more peaceful moods, flocks of coots are often seen grazing quietly on grassy banks near the water.

About eight kinds of coots are found around the world. All of them are slate-gray to blackish, with large, pale bills, and all are immediately recognizable as members of this group. One of the strangest of the lot is the giant coot (*Fulica gigantea*), found only around lakes at very high elevations in the Andes.

Somewhere between the secretive nature of the rails and the brazen open-water existence of the coots is the life-style of the gallinules and moorhens. These birds are shaped like coots, but are often more colorful, sometimes marked with iridescent blues, purples, and greens in the plumage, and bright colors on the bill and legs. A good example of this group is the American purple gallinule (*Porphyrula martinica*), a gaudy resident of marshes in the southern United States and the tropics. Purple gallinules can swim quite well, and often do; but more of their time is spent stalking about in the marsh, walking on floating vegetation, or climbing in the branches of bushes and trees above the water. When swimming, gallinules and moorhens usually stay close to the protection of marsh vegetation, not venturing out into the middle of large open lakes the way coots often do.

On our first view of a rail, seeing it flutter away low over the marsh, it seems hard to believe that these birds could migrate any distance. Yet some species regularly migrate hundreds, even thousands of miles. Some soras, for example, fly to South America every fall, and back north to the United States or Canada in spring; some European rails spend every winter in central Africa. These migration routes force the birds to cross large expanses of open water, and those heading south into Africa must cross the Sahara Desert—hardly an inviting place for a marsh bird. So it is clear that some rails are capable of making lengthy, sustained flights.

Rails are also capable of making big mistakes. There are a number of cases on record of rails turning up thousands of miles from where they are "supposed" to occur. Scientists were nonplussed when a spotted rail (*Pardirallus maculatus*) from the American tropics was found dead in Pennsylvania in 1976. The next year another one was found in Texas, and the year after that, a South American rail called the paint-billed crake (*Neocrex erythrops*) was found in Virginia. The North American sora has appeared in Europe several times.

Many migrating birds save energy by flying downwind: they wait until the wind is blowing in the direction that they intend to go. Rails, short-winged fliers that they are, may be especially reliant on such tail winds. And if the wind shifts and the rail is swept off course, its best chance for survival may be to continue flying downwind rather than to fight the gales. This factor could explain why so many oceanic islands have rails: all over the Pacific, the South Atlantic, and the Indian Ocean, there are islands that have their own localized rail species. Each of these must represent some event in the past when a group of lost rails found the island, found each other, and established a colony.

On islands where there were no predators, rails would have had no real need to fly. In fact, birds living on small islands in large oceans could find that flight was positively dangerous, as there would be the possibility of being blown out to sea. Thus many of the island species of rails have gradually lost the ability to fly. This adaptation has had tragic results in a number of cases, where man has accidentally brought predators such as rats or snakes to these isolated islands; several of these special island rails have become extinct. Among the losses were two birds from the Hawaiian Islands, the Laysan rail (*Porzanula palmeri*) and the Hawaii rail (*Pennula sandwichensis*).

Of course, many birds besides rails live in marshes, and there are a few small families of birds that specialize in this habitat. The three species of screamers in South America represent one such family, the Anhimidae. Screamers are actually related to ducks, but in appearance they suggest stocky, strong-legged, aquatic chickens. Although they often seem secretive, hiding in marshy or swampy places, screamers will sometimes soar about over open country. They earn their group name with a variety of ear-splitting shrieks, honks, and trumpeting sounds.

Perhaps the most graceful of all marsh birds are the members of the jacana family (Jacanidae), a small group related to the sandpipers. These birds, found in all the tropical regions of the world, are marked by their very long—almost absurdly long—toes. This adaptation distributes the birds' weight so well that they can walk on lily pads and other flimsy pieces of floating vegetation. Nicknames like "lily-trotter" or "water-walker" are often applied to them.

Jacanas are usually found fairly near dense marshes, to which they can retreat if danger is imminent. But most of the time they are out walking about in the open, so it would be pointless for them to wear cryptic camouflage; most have bright colors and striking patterns, often with colorful lobes or wattles around the base of the bill, and contrasting patches of color in the wings.

The parent bird that does the incubating is usually the male, because in most species of jacanas, the sex roles are reversed from their usual order in the bird world. Females are usually larger than males, and after they lay the eggs, the male does the work of hatching the eggs and caring for the young. The northern jacana (*Jacana spinosa*) is found from southern Texas to Panama; it is only "northern" by comparison to the wattled jacana (*Jacana jacana*) of South America; in these species, each female may have three or four mates, laying her eggs in nests built by each.

Similar habits are practiced by the pheasant-tailed jacana (*Hydrophasianus chirurgus*) of southern Asia. A female of this species may lay as many as ten clutches of eggs in a season, with various males in her territory taking the responsibility for bringing up the baby jacanas. But even without these noteworthy marital relations the pheasant-tailed jacana would be an impressive bird, with its broad white wings, long flowing tail, and elegant color pattern. It is perhaps the most beautiful of all the remarkable birds that live in the marshes of the world.

Opposite and overleaf. Coots are ducklike members of the rail family. Buoyant swimmers and fair divers, they are propelled by lobed or webbed toes similar to those of grebes. The American coot (Fulica americana), *which breeds from Canada to South America, raises as many as ten chicks every year. The black down of the precocial young is accented by a red bill, a red bald spot on the head, and a scattering of curly red and orange hairs. The chicks' stubby wings have pronounced claws that help them maneuver through the dense vegetation near the nest. Coots dive to depths of twenty-five feet to feed on submerged plants; they can remain underwater for as long as sixteen seconds.* (Tim Fitzharris; Carroll W. Perkins)

Right. *A cosmopolitan inhabitant of freshwater marshes and lakes, the common moorhen (Gallinula* chloropus) *indeed suggests a plump chicken as it cackles about the cattails.* (Arthur Morris)

Top two rows. *Many marsh-dwelling birds have long toes that enable them to walk about on flimsy lily pads and other floating vegetation. Since no other birds can enter this specialized habitat, these birds have exclusive foraging rights. A few rails, including the sora and some gallinules, also have this specialized feature, but most of these long-toed birds are members of the jacana family, akin to the shorebirds.*

From the top row at the left to the bottom row at the right, the birds are a sora (Porzana carolina), *an African jacana* (Actophilornis africanus), *an Australian jacana or lotusbird* (Irediparra gallinacea), *a northern jacana* (Jacana spinosa) *from Central America, an American purple gallinule* (Porphyrula martinica), *and a pheasant-tailed jacana* (Hydrophasianus chirurgus) *from tropical Asia.* (Jeff Foott; Hans D. Dossenbach; Glen Threlfo/Auscape International; Anthony Mercieca; Jack Dermid; Eric Hosking)

Overleaf. *As if posing for an official family portrait, with a lotus blossom as their emblem behind them, a brood of young lotusbirds stand on lily pads in Queensland, Australia. The toes may seem long in these downy young birds, but in the heavier adults, the toes are even longer. Lotusbirds breed from Borneo eastward through Indonesia to the tropical parts of Australia.* (Glen Threlfo/Auscape International)

Below. *Bursting from a pond with a fish in its sharp-pointed bill, a European kingfisher (Alcedo atthis) will return to a favorite perch, beat its catch against a branch, then swallow the fish headfirst. When it spies a fish in the water below its perch, the kingfisher plummets at a forty-five-degree angle with powerful wingbeats, adjusting its aim at the last instant by fanning its tail feathers, and seizing the prey with eyes closed! Scientists divide the kingfishers into two groups—fishing kingfishers and forest kingfishers, most of which never go near water but hunt frogs, lizards, centipedes, and snakes.* (Heintges/Zefa/National Audubon Society Collection, Photo Researchers, Inc.)

A Bright Rainbow of Kingfishers

As we walk beside the river, our attention is caught by a loud, rattling call. Turning to find the source of the sound, we see a chunky, large-billed bird, patterned in blue-gray and white, flying over the river. Suddenly the bird pauses and hovers in one spot on rapidly beating wings, looking down at the water; then it plummets toward the surface. Its plunge looks clumsy and unpracticed—but after a brief splash, the bird rises and flies away, carrying a fish in its bill.

The bird is a belted kingfisher (*Ceryle alcyon*), and it is one of the most familiar denizens of the water's edge throughout North America. We could travel from Alaska to Florida, from California to Quebec, and everywhere we would see this bird —and no other sorts of kingfishers. Such a journey would not give us any hint of what a diverse and colorful group the kingfisher family (Alcedinidae) is in the rest of the world.

Viewed alone, here in the land where it is the only kingfisher, the belted serves as a fair introduction to its family. It is a medium-sized bird, not much bigger than a blue jay (*Cyanocitta cristata*) in body size, but with a larger head and a much longer, heavier bill. By contrast, its feet are relatively small and its legs are short. Most kingfishers have some elongated head feathers, creating at least a slightly crested effect, although the belted kingfisher carries this to an extreme with a shaggy, double-peaked mop of a crest. Like most members of its family, the belted kingfisher is a solitary bird: it is seen singly or in pairs, never in flocks. Its voice is loud, harsh, and very distinctive. It hunts by plunging bill-first into the water, either from an exposed perch or after hovering, having spotted likely prey at or just below the surface. Putting its large bill to another use, it digs horizontal tunnels for nesting in vertical banks of soil.

There is reason to believe that the kingfishers came to their role as water birds somewhat late in their development. No other bird family thought to be closely related to the kingfishers is associated with water in anything more than the most incidental way. Instead, the common theme for many of these groups—such exotic, mostly tropical families as the rollers (Coraciidae), bee-eaters (Meropidae), and todies (Todidae)—is the habit of watching from a perch and flying out to catch insects, lizards, and other creatures.

At some point in the distant past, some ancestral member of this clan must have noticed that life was abundant just below the surface of the water in shallow streams—must have found that a deft flier could snatch minnows from the water without actually having to submerge or even get very wet. Fishing from the air obviously turned out to be a productive niche, and the kingfishers prospered.

But if these flying fishermen evolved from birds that originally hunted away from the water, it seems that some kingfishers eventually traveled this evolutionary road back in the opposite direction, as we shall see later.

In the New World, variety in this family begins to pick up in southern Texas. The pint-sized green kingfisher (*Chloroceryle americana*) is found there, perching low on stones and twigs close to the water, watching for minnows and aquatic insects. So is the ringed kingfisher (*Ceryle torquata*); this bigger, clatter-voiced edition of the belted often flies high, perches high, and dives for larger fish. Continuing south into the tropics, three more species of New World kingfishers appear, each of a slightly different size and habitat preference. The belted kingfisher is only a winter visitor to the tropics, but there are places where all five of the others can be found regularly in the same general area.

Researchers in South America have found that where more different kinds of kingfishers share the same waters, each tends to be more specialized in its habits than in areas where there are fewer kingfisher species. Competition may force them to be more selective in how high above the water they perch, what size of prey they take, and so on. Or, to put it another way, being more specialized may allow them to avoid direct competition. But for more species to be "packed in" this way, the available food must be abundant and varied.

Calling the roll of the kingfishers, we can check off the six kinds found in North and South America. How many are left, elsewhere in the world? More than eighty! The Old World is clearly the place to go for kingfisher diversity.

Europe, like most of North America, has only one species. British bird watchers call it simply "the kingfisher"; scientists call it the European kingfisher (*Alcedo atthis*), and across all of Europe and vast areas of northern and central Asia it is the only member of its family. Living along small brooks and ponds as well as larger rivers in the European countryside, it is only half the size of the belted kingfisher. However, it is much more colorful: it has bright red feet, orange underparts, and brilliant blue and green on the back. It is, in fact, more brightly colored than any kingfishers of the Americas, and it serves as a good introduction to its family in the Old World.

All of the fifteen African members of the family are immediately recognizable as being similar in form to the belted and European kingfishers. Most of them are similar in habits as well. For example, the gemlike little malachite kingfisher (*Alcedo cristata*), found throughout much of Africa, is a permanent resident of the waterside, where it perches on low branches and reeds and often dives for insect larvae.

But other African species are willing to take their insects on the wing, or from the ground, and thus they are able to forage away from the water. A couple of small kingfishers that inhabit deep forests in equatorial Africa are said to feed largely upon crickets. Altogether more than half the African species in the family are known to spend at least part of their time foraging away from water. Some, such as the striped kingfisher (*Halcyon chelicuti*), are characteristic of dry woodland and savanna, and they feed entirely upon insects and lizards. Hearing the shrill "referee-whistle" call of this bird in the dry thorn scrub, far from water, the visitor may have a hard time at first believing that this voice is that of a kingfisher.

The greatest development of variety in this family is in the region known as Australasia, which stretches from southern Asia to Australia and includes the thousands of islands, large and small, that lie between these two land masses. More than sixty species of kingfishers, fully three-fourths of the family, can be found in this area, although some are more widespread and occur in other places as well.

The kingfishers of this part of the world are particularly notable not only for the number of species, but also for their many extreme variations in form and habits. A widespread bird in this region is the stork-billed kingfisher (*Pelargopsis capensis*), found from India to the Philippines, with over a dozen local varieties on islands such as Borneo and Java. As its name suggests, it has a huge, bright red bill, out of all proportion to the size of the rest of the bird.

Among the most famous members of the family (although few people realize that these birds are kingfishers) is the laughing kookaburra (*Dacelo gigas*) of Australia. Kookaburras are large, stout-billed birds, about a foot and a half in length, that live in small groups in semi-open country. They hunt lizards, large insects, and even snakes, watching for them from high perches and then swooping in to attack. But their notoriety comes from their incredible vocal performances: as three or four kookaburras perch close together on a snag, one begins with a low, evil-sounding chuckle. The others join in and the sound becomes a loud, discordant cackle, increasing in volume until the birds are almost shrieking. Seemingly inspired by their efforts, other groups in the distance will take up the chorus, until the countryside echoes with the raucous laughter of the kookaburras.

North of Australia lies New Guinea, one of the world's largest islands. New Guinea could be considered the heart of the Australasian region, and it is definitely the center of diversity for the kingfisher clan. More than twenty species are found on this one island—more than on the whole continent of Africa. The kingfishers of New Guinea are a varied lot, and they illustrate the concept of adaptive radiation. In the isolation of this island, where they apparently arrived before many other families of birds, the relative lack of competition allowed them to adapt to many niches that they do not occupy elsewhere.

As a result, it is very difficult to generalize about New Guinea's kingfishers. Some are musical. The blue-black kingfisher (*Halcyon nigrocyanea*), for example, has a whistled song with a clear, sweet quality. Some are comfortable in the dark: the hook-billed kingfisher (*Melidora macrorrhina*), which has an abrupt downcurved hook at the tip of its bill, lives in the shadows of New Guinea's deep forest, and is active mostly at dawn and dusk; it may even hunt at night. And others are coastal: the beach kingfisher (*Halcyon saurophaga*) and the collared kingfisher (*Halcyon chloris*) are almost never found inland. They hug the immediate coast of New Guinea, swooping out to capture crabs on the beach or small fish in saltwater channels through the mangroves.

Some New Guinea kingfishers have diverse nesting sites; although there are some that nest in holes in dirt banks, like most family members elsewhere, there are others that nest in holes in trees or in holes excavated in termite mounds.

Kingfishers come in a wide range of sizes, too. Some are huge: New Guinea has three species of kookaburras, including the blue-winged (*Dacelo leachii*), which is nearly as large as the laughing kookaburra of Australia. Some are tiny: the aptly named little kingfisher (*Alcedo pusilla*) is practically as small as a hummingbird. Only slightly larger is the dwarf kingfisher (*Ceyx lepidus*), which is sometimes seen hunting for insects in the branches of tall forest trees.

The shovel-billed kingfisher (*Clytoceyx rex*) of New Guinea's forest is probably the oddest member of the family. Its bill is short and very heavy, appearing in profile like a shovel blade turned up on edge. The bird uses this blunt instrument to dig in the soil for insects, grubs, and earthworms. What a contrast to its gorgeous cousins, the paradise kingfishers (*Tanysiptera*), which may be the most beautiful of the whole colorful clan. New Guinea has half a dozen kinds of paradise kingfishers. All have bright red bills and brilliant blue in the plumage, and all have extra-long central tail feathers patterned in blue and white. To go with their exotic appearance, they give a variety of musical trilled calls. They dig their nesting tunnels in active termite mounds, and the birds may be seen anywhere in the interior of the forest, including high up in the trees and far from water.

As a family, the kingfishers are not typical water birds. But they certainly add color and interest to the waterside—and other habitats—around the world.

Opposite and overleaf. Like a gleaming blue butterfly with long white tail feathers, a buff-breasted paradise kingfisher (Tanysiptera sylvia) *flutters through the dark rain forests of Queensland, Australia, plucking up insects, frogs, snails, and lizards from branches and the ground. The two tail streamers, which are in constant motion even when the bird is perched, give the bird an overall length of about twelve inches. These kingfishers are active birds, quickly changing position on a perch. At one moment, you are likely to see the black-and-blue back and wings, and then in a twinkling of an eye, the bird has flipped around, revealing the rich buff color of the breast that gives this bird its name.* (Clifford B. Frith/Bruce Coleman, Inc.; Ralph and Daphne Keller/NHPA)

Above. *Few of the world's birds are as colorful as the many species of kingfishers that inhabit the tropical forests and rivers of Africa and southern Asia. They come in several shades of brilliant blue, often have spangled crests, which the birds raise and lower frequently, and the face and breast may be buff or even delicate violet. Their bills are usually red or orange, and of different shapes, each one an adaptation for capturing a particular kind of small prey. Stout-billed species tend to take larger prey, and small-billed ones specialize in tiny minnows.*

From top left to bottom right, the species here are the African malachite kingfisher (Alcedo cristata), *the related Malagasy kingfisher* (Alcedo vintsioides) *of Madagascar, the stork-billed kingfisher* (Pelargopsis capensis) *of coastal Asian mangroves, and the pygmy kingfisher* (Ceyx pictus) *of Africa.* (Peter Johnson/NHPA; H. Uible/National Audubon Society Collection, Photo Researchers, Inc.; Frank W. Lane/Bruce Coleman, Inc.; M.P.L. Fogden/Bruce Coleman, Inc.)

231

Above and opposite. *A male European kingfisher successfully courts a mate by offering her a fish with its head toward her. The pair's territory will extend 125 yards above and below their streamside nest site, and they will defend it with vigor. To start a tunnel, the birds fly straight into a steep bank, knocking out clumps of dirt with their beaks. Once the hole is deep enough for a toehold, they shovel out earth with their feet until they have dug an upward-sloping tunnel two to three feet long. European kingfishers raise six to eight young, each requiring half a dozen fish a day.* (Guenter Ziesler)

Overleaf. *Largest of its family is the giant kingfisher* (Ceryle maxima)—*eighteen inches long with a wingspan of twenty-eight inches. The giant kingfisher haunts forested rivers and pools across most of Africa, but nowhere is it a common bird. A pair will watch a favorite fishing spot from dawn to dusk, carrying food to the three nestlings that wait in a muddy chamber at the end of an eight-foot-long riverbank tunnel.* (M. Philip Kahl/National Audubon Society Collection, Photo Researchers, Inc.)

Below. *A familiar sight near rivers, lakes, and swamps everywhere south of the Sahara, the African fishing eagle* (Haliaeetus vocifer) *is a noisy bird, shrieking its five-syllable* weeah-hya-hya-hya *from dawn to dusk, on the wing or from a perch. Indeed, in the words of one noted ornithologist, the fishing eagle is "the voice of Africa." Having sighted a fish in the water below, this bird slips quietly from a branch in a dead tree beside the Okavango River in Botswana. As it descends swiftly toward the water, it keeps its eyes fixed on its prey.* (Peter Johnson/NHPA)

Aquatic Hunters

The world's abundance of birds is integrated into nearly every kind of habitat on the planet. We have seen through these pages the most aquatic of all birds, such as the penguins and the grebes, and we have seen the greatest ocean voyagers, the tubenoses. We have looked at the teeming wealth of bird life along our shores, and in our marshes and shallows. We have seen a spectrum of life-styles ranging from broadly generalized opportunism, which is the calling of many gulls, to the striking specialization of the knife-billed skimmers or the open-billed storks. From flightless rails and steamer-ducks to the champions of long-distance migration among the shearwaters and terns, from a solitary existence to life in colonies a million birds strong, we have hinted at the astounding range of adaptations to be found among water birds.

Yet three quarters of the world's modern bird families do not contain aquatic species. Water is essential in the economy and the annual cycle of every bird, and relatively few can exist in the complete absence of water, but birds are by and large creatures of the earth's terrestrial habitats. It bespeaks, therefore, the lure of the water that even among many primarily terrestrial families of birds there are representatives that have ventured back into its realm. As we saw in the preceding chapter, a number of the kingfishers obtain their food almost exclusively by plunging into the water for fish and other prey.

Among the songbirds, one group of plump, thrushlike birds has evolved an aquatic existence. These are the dippers (family Cinclidae); they are at home in swift-flowing streams, where they feed on insect eggs and larvae and other items on rocky bottoms. Quite unusual members of the order Passeriformes—the perching birds—the dippers spend much time completely submerged. In southeastern Asia, another group of songbirds, thrushes known as forktails (*Enicurus*), is also partial to flowing streams; they derive much of their food from rocky stream bottoms, and sometimes enter the water in the manner of a dipper. And along the windswept coastlines of southern South America the seaside cinclodes (*Cinclodes nigrofumosus*), a chunky robin-sized passerine, feeds freely on marine invertebrates among the rocks and floating kelp; its is a soggy existence for birds in an otherwise terrestrial family, the Furnariidae, or ovenbirds.

It is among the large, predatory birds—the owls, hawks, and eagles—that hunting in the water has evolved in the most dramatic fashion. We have seen, through these chapters, a variety of tactics employed by water birds for catching fish and other aquatic prey. Bills have evolved into virtually every conceivable kind of fish-catching apparatus. Yet none of these birds, from pelican to heron, or from cormorant to gull, uses its feet to capture prey. The use of talons to grasp prey is the trademark of the owls (family Strigidae), barn-owls (Tytonidae), falcons (Falconidae), and hawks and eagles (Accipitridae). In a few species of hawks and owls, fishing has become the predominant way of life. In this final chapter we will examine those predators that depend upon aquatic ecosystems, but have their home base upon the land.

Owls are finely adapted creatures of the night. Densely packed rods on the retinas of their large, forward-facing eyes give them acute vision in very dim light, and a keen sense of hearing allows some species to locate prey even in total darkness. Soft-edged flight feathers allow most owls to fly with a ghostly silence. Attuned to the night, owls employ additional adaptations to capture their prey—such as a strong, hooked bill and powerful feet with sharp talons; these adaptations closely parallel the features of hawks, eagles, and falcons.

A diet of fish has become the livelihood of two small groups of owls, both restricted to the Old World. In all, seven species of "fish-owls" are divided between the Asiatic genus *Ketupa* and the African genus *Scotopelia*. Successful fish-owls must not only locate fish, but must also capture and hold on to them. It appears that these birds locate fish visually, scanning the water for prey from riverside perches on branches or tree stumps. The owls then fly low over the water, swooping to snatch fish from the surface. The legs of fish-owls are relatively long and, unlike those of their closest relatives, are completely unfeathered along the tarsus. The powerful curved claws are excellent fish hooks. But holding on to a slippery, wriggling fish is no easy trick, and the fish-owls cope with this problem with a remarkable adaptation on the soles of their large feet: sharp, spike-like scales, packed abundantly and projecting at different angles. With this roughness, the feet are astonishingly similar to those of the most highly adapted of the fish-eating hawks, the osprey (*Pandion haliaetus*); this similarity is a good example of the principle of convergence, which we also saw in the loons and grebes.

There are no specialized fish-eating owls in the Americas; this is the sort of biogeographical quirk that stimulates wonder and theorizing among evolutionary biologists—though in such musings, simple answers are rarely found. There are specialized fish-eating bats in the New World, but these are localized coastal animals and thus not likely to have prevented, through nighttime competition, the evolution or immigration of fishing owls.

The worldwide distribution of the falcons, hawks, eagles, and their relatives has spawned a diverse array of hunting techniques inflicted upon a similarly diverse spectrum of prey. From deft and dainty insect-eating kites and small falcons to rain forest eagles that prey on twenty-pound mammals, these raptors are the dominant daytime hunting birds of terrestrial environments. Many raptors derive some of their prey from wetland habitats—the harriers, for example, which hunt over marshes—but only in a few genera of hawks and eagles do we find species that capture prey directly out of the water. The most specialized of all is the osprey, as its moniker "fish hawk" suggests.

The osprey is one of the most cosmopolitan birds of prey, breeding widely in the Northern Hemisphere and also in a few regions of the Southern Hemisphere. Many northern populations are highly migratory. Except when migrating, ospreys are seldom found far from water, for it is from lakes, reservoirs, estuaries, and sea coasts that they derive their food. Outwardly, ospreys differ little from the hawks and eagles, but an examination of their feet reveals the fishing equipment. Like the feet of the fish-owls, an osprey's feet have scales modified as sharp spicules; these spicules work with the strong talons to ensure a grasp on even the most slippery of fish. Coursing over the water's surface, ospreys spot their prey with keen eyesight and go after it feetfirst, making quite a splash, with feet down and wings up. In productive fishing waters, an osprey's success would be the envy of any fisherman.

After a successful fishing foray, the osprey carries its prey in its talons to a feeding site or its nest. None of the fish-eating seabirds has this ability; they must instead carry prey in their bill, pouch, or esophagus. Ospreys nest in a variety of situations that meet two main requirements: safety from predators, and a reasonable commuting distance to fishing waters. Their stick nests may be built high in trees or even directly on the ground; along some coastlines, as in Baja California, ospreys sometimes nest in colonies.

The familiar bald eagle (*Haliaeetus leucocephalus*) of North America is one of eight "sea eagles," a group of large, powerful raptors that feed to a varying extent upon fish and other aquatic creatures. Bald eagles use a strong sweep of their powerful feet and talons to pick dead or living fish from the surface; though they rarely plunge into the water, they do have limited, if awkward, swimming abilities, and can use their broad wings to row. Close relatives of the bald eagle include the African fishing eagle (*Haliaeetus vocifer*), a noisy and conspicuous bird of Africa's tropical lakes and rivers, and the huge and spectacular Steller's sea eagle (*Haliaeetus pelagicus*) of the Korean and Siberian coasts.

Some sea eagles, notably the white-bellied sea eagle (*Haliaeetus leucogaster*) of the coasts of India, southeast Asia, and Australia, supplement their fish diet with sea snakes. Fishing is also the way of life of the two species of fishing eagles of southeastern Asia. Living up to their generic name *Ichthyophaga* ("fish-eater"), these birds inhabit streamside forests, using their long talons and scaly feet to catch and hold freshwater fish.

The fishing eagles, sea eagles, fishing owls, and the osprey represent a highly evolved intersection of predatory habit and aquatic habitat. Theirs is an interplay of form, function, and environment repeated in family after family of birds, from penguins and petrels to kingfishers and dippers.

Late on a Florida afternoon, the hot and damp air hangs still over an expanse of marsh. Water and sawgrass combine and roll into the distance in a dance of heat waves; the outlines of palms and a jungle growth of trees interrupt the horizon. The heavy air is cut by a line of white ibis (*Eudocimus albus*) over the marsh; below them, pockets of herons, wood storks (*Mycteria americana*), and ibises methodically search a pool of water for food. A bald eagle courses the distance between palm hammocks, and ahead of it ducks spring into flight, grebes dive under the water with quick forward flips, and rails grind out their calls from the hiding places in the marsh vegetation.

A different bird of prey appears low over the marsh, flapping and sailing on broad, slate-black wings, its wide white tail base flashing conspicuously. A quick maneuver brings the raptor to the water's edge, where its talons gain a sure and deadly grasp on an apple snail (*Pomacea*). The snail is carried some distance to the stub of a long-drowned tree.

The bird is a snail kite (*Rostrhamus sociabilis*), a member of the hawk and eagle family with a specialized calling—capturing and eating apple snails. Common in South America, and found locally north to eastern Mexico, Cuba, and southern Florida, the snail kite uses its thin, hooklike upper mandible in tandem with its grasping, sharp-clawed feet to extract the snail from its shell. As our bird accomplishes this trick, the meat of the snail impaled on its bill, the empty shell tumbles to the ground, joining a hundred others as a legacy of the kite's adeptness at its narrow specialty.

Across the marsh, from a hammock's edge, the wailing cry of a limpkin (*Aramus guarauna*) cuts through the warm, still air. This is the long-legged stalker that we met in the first chapter; like the kite, the limpkin has just dined on apple snails. Two birds of different form and different ancestries, converging in a single specialization. These are just two birds among a fascinating and diverse spectrum of species that live in and around the most precious of our earth's resources: water.

Opposite. *As the fishing eagle rushes toward the fish it has sighted, streaking along only inches above the surface, it swings its legs forward and opens razor-sharp talons. At this point in the plummeting attack, the bird goes on "automatic pilot," for in the final seconds of its flight, the fishing eagle can no longer see its intended victim. The eagle pulls its head back to protect its eyes from injury, and brings the talons into the position its last view showed would mean a successful strike. During these few blind seconds, the fish has a chance to dart quickly to safety.* (F.S. Mitchell/Tom Stack and Associates)

Above. *The African fishing eagle has scored a direct hit, and snatches the fish from the surface without even wetting its feathers. Where fish are abundant, fishing eagles are gregarious; in one location, nine pairs occupied a 500-acre island. The African fishing eagle is not the only African bird that takes fish from the water's surface. The black kite* (Milvus migrans), *found throughout most of the Old World, is an expert fish-catcher, as well as a pirate, scavenger, and general predator, fearlessly entering towns in pursuit of poultry, rats, and even garbage.* (Arthur Gloor/Animals, Animals; Tom Nebbia)

Opposite. *The world's most widespread fish-eating raptor is the osprey* (Pandion haliaetus), *found on every continent except Antarctica. It usually hovers in the air over the water, and then catches its prey in spectacular splashing dives.* (Laura Riley)

Overleaves. *Our national bird, the bald eagle* (Haliaeetus leucocephalus) *often catches fish, but also obtains much of its food by robbing the smaller osprey of its catch. Pesticides in the fish brought the bald eagle to the threshold of extinction, but now that most of these chemicals have been banned, this noble bird is recovering.* (Jeff Foott; R.H. Armstrong/Animals, Animals)

Notes on Photographers

Robert H. Armstrong, a former Fisheries Biologist for the Alaska Department of Fish and Game, has been awarded an honorary doctorate from the University of Alaska.

Yann Arthus-Bertrand is a French photographer who lived and worked in Kenya for three years. He is the author of six books, including *Lion*.

Michel Bourque studied veterinary medicine in school, and has been a nature photographer for more than twenty years, traveling to South and Central America with his camera.

Fred Bruemmer is a writer and photographer, specializing in arctic and antarctic regions. He was awarded the Order of Canada for his studies of the peoples of the North.

Gay Bumgarner is a landscape designer and photographer. Her articles have been published in *Flower and Garden* and *American Horticulturist*.

John Cancalosi is the founder and director of Vida Nature Series, which produces educational programs on wildlife shown in schools in Arizona, Colorado, and Wyoming.

Jean-Claude Carton is a French photographer and part-time drawing teacher. His work has won several international prizes.

Jack Dermid, a former professor at the University of North Carolina, is now devoting his time to photography and writing. His work has appeared in *National Geographic*.

Larry R. Ditto is a wildlife refuge manager for the U.S. Fish and Wildlife Services. His work has appeared in *Audubon* and *Natural History*.

Hans D. Dossenbach and his family live in a three hundred year-old Swiss farmhouse. He has worked as a naturalist and photographer, and has published twenty-five books.

Jon Farrar is the senior editor of *Nebraskaland* magazine. His photographs have been used in many magazines and books, including the Audubon Society field guides.

Jean-Paul Ferrero, a photographer himself, moved from France to Australia where he founded Auscape International, a photo agency specializing in Australian subjects.

Tim Fitzharris is the author and photographer of six natural history books. He is an instructor of photography at Cornell University's Laboratory of Ornithology.

M.P.L. Fogden is a professional biologist with a doctorate in ornithology from Oxford. He is co-author (with his wife) of *Animals and their Colours*.

Jeff Foott has been a marine biologist, mountain-climbing guide, member of the National Ski Patrol, and National Park Ranger, as well as a wildlife photographer and film-maker.

Clifford B. Frith has an extensive background in zoology and ecology, especially concerning birds and reptiles. He is a full-time photographer, and has traveled worldwide.

Arthur Gloor taught himself to be a nature photographer. He runs a safari business in Namibia and Botswana, which gives him ample opportunity for photography.

François Gohier is a French photographer who has lived in North and South America for the past several years. His work appeared in *The Audubon Society Book of Wild Cats*.

Ben Goldstein is a retired chemist who photographs birds. He has traveled to Norway and the Seychelles for his subjects, and his work has been published in *National Wildlife*.

Chuck Gordon spent thirteen years with the Canadian Wildlife Service. His work has been used by the Alberta government and the National Museums of Canada.

Heintges takes wildlife pictures for esthetic reasons, not biological ones. He heats a pond on his property in the winter and photographs the birds that come to feed.

Irene Hinke Sacilotto has photographed the wildlife of North America and Africa. Her work has been published in *Defenders* and *Natural History*.

Eric Hosking is a British photographer whose career spans several decades. He has traveled on expeditions ranging from Antarctica to Greenland and the Canadian Arctic. He was awarded the O.B.E. in 1977.

Peter Johnson has been honored by photographic institutes internationally. He is a member of the Explorers Club, and has published eight books.

Janos Jurka began his career as a nature photographer in 1960 in Sweden. He has mounted two exhibitions of his photography.

M. Philip Kahl's work has been reproduced in *National Geographic*. He holds a doctorate in zoology, and has studied storks and flamingos for over twenty years.

Robert Y. Kaufman is a retired U.S. Navy Vice Admiral, who left the Navy to see the world as a wildlife photographer. He is currently completing books on Alaska and submarines.

Steven C. Kaufman worked as a park ranger and for a seismic exploration company in the arctic before becoming a full-time photographer. His work has appeared in *Geo*.

Ralph and Daphne Keller have a special fascination for north Queensland, Australia's tropical rain forests, and have spent two years photographing the wildlife there.

G.C. Kelley has been taking pictures for natural history publications for over twenty years. He travels extensively for his subjects, and has been published in *Audubon*.

Frank W. Lane concentrates on zoo photography, and has amassed a collection of rare animals on film. He founded the Frank Lane Picture Agency, and wrote *The Violent Earth*.

Wayne Lankinen lives in South Gillies, Ontario. Birds are the usual subject of his photographs, which have been published in *Nature Canada*, *Audubon*, and *The Living Bird*.

Tom and Pat Leeson specialize in photographing wildlife of the western United States. Their work is frequently seen in *Smithsonian* and *Natural History*.

Douglas Leighton was a Park Naturalist in Canada for eight years. He is now a freelance photographer and writer, and a regular contributor to *Nature Canada*.

T.N. Liversedge is a biologist and photographer, who spent two years in the Okavango Delta in Botswana gathering information on the rare Pel's fishing-owl.

Barry W. Mansell has photographed Florida wildlife for eighteen years, and his work has appeared in biological textbooks and presentations for environmental protection.

Anthony Mercieca immigrated to the United States from Malta in 1959.

His subjects range from copepods in the oceans to bighorn sheep on mountaintops and everything in between.

Michael and Irene Morcombe live in Western Australia, and are the authors of *Australia: The Wild Continent*.

C. Allan Morgan specializes in photographing animals of the western United States and Mexico. He also leads natural history and whale-watching tours in Baja California.

Arthur Morris is a fledgling photographer, whose work has been widely published. He is in charge of the shorebird survey at the Jamaica Bay Wildlife Refuge in New York City.

Tom Nebbia freelances for *National Geographic*, whose assignments have sent him to such places as Germany and Botswana.

Roland Nilsson spends his free time photographing nature, especially birds and wildflowers. During the winter he travels and lectures on nature and conservation efforts.

Dr. John F. O'Connor is Associate Dean and a professor at the Boston University School of Medicine. His lifelong interest in wildlife and environmental issues led him to become a director of the Massachusetts Audubon Society.

Tom W. Parkin worked as a naturalist in the parks of Canada before turning to photography. He has won awards from Canadian and American conservation organizations.

Carroll Perkins is especially interested the natural history of the tropics. He specializes in photographing birds, insects, wildflowers, and fungi.

Rod Planck became interested in water birds at the age of nine. He hopes that his photography will interest others in nature and protecting the environment.

C. Gable Ray has a special interest in waterfowl and photographs natural history subjects exclusively. His pictures have been seen in Sierra Club calendars.

Laura Riley's work has appeared in magazines from *Defenders* to *Forbes*. She co-authored *Guide to the National Wildlife Refuges*, nominated for a Pulitzer Prize.

Peter Roberts runs a stock photography business in Seattle. His work has appeared in such magazines as *Living Bird* and *Natural History*.

Graham Robertson is a biologist with the National Parks and Wildlife Service in Australia. He has written scientific papers on penguins, and is writing a book on albatrosses.

Brian M. Rogers is a family doctor by profession, but he has photographed wildlife from East Africa to South America. His particular interest is in rain forests.

Lynn Rogers holds a Ph.D. in wildlife ecology and behavior. His specialty is North American wildlife, and his photo credits include *National Geographic* and *National Wildlife*.

Leonard Lee Rue III is the author of twenty books, and his work has appeared regularly in *Audubon*, *Natural History*, and *Newsweek*.

Klas Rune is a trained biologist, and his work has been published in such magazines as *Geo*. He has written two books about the Swedish seacoast.

Kevin Schafer worked as a biologist on the Farallon Islands studying the breeding of Cassin's auklets. He is now a full-time photographer, and has been published in *Outside*.

Joy Spurr has over thirty years' experience as photographer, writer, and lecturer on nature subjects. Her photographs have been seen in Taylor's Guide to Gardening Series.

Alvin E. Staffan has been a nature artist and photographer for thirty-five years. His photographs have appeared in all major natural history magazines.

Lynn Stone considers himself a naturalist, and writes about wildlife as well as photographing it. His children's books cover topics from birds of prey to endangered animals.

Gary Strassler started by photographing sports, and has covered skiing championships and bicycle races. He now devotes his time to nature and wildlife photography.

Charles G. Summers, Jr., was named Wildlife Photographer of the Year in 1985 by the British Museum (Natural History).

Rita Summers was a winner in *National Wildlife's* photo contest in 1984 and 1985. She and her husband, Charles, lead photographic safaris to Africa, and publish *Phototrak*.

Karl H. Switak has traveled from New Guinea to Africa's Namib Desert photographing natural history subjects.

Glen Threlfo lives and works as a guide in Lamington National Park, Queensland, Australia. He concentrates on photographing rainforest wildlife.

Frank S. Todd spent thirteen seasons in Antarctica, and was awarded the National Science Foundation's U.S. Polar Medal. He now works on breeding animals in captivity.

Jean-Philippe Varin is a French biologist and photographer. He founded Jacana, an international nature photography agency, and is co-author of *Photographing Wildlife*.

Robert Villani is a wildlife artist and photographer, specializing in birds. He is an avid backpacker who has completed hikes of the Appalachian and Vermont Long trails.

Larry West is a naturalist and photographer. His work has been published in *Audubon, Natural History* and *National Geographic*.

Manfred Wiechmann lives in West Germany. He is primarily interested in water birds, and he was the first to capture on film the egg-laying behavior of the great crested grebe.

Steve Wilson attempts through films and widely published photographs to increase man's awareness of the other living things on our planet.

Art Wolfe is a photographer and a painter. In 1981 and 1982 the Frye Art Museum in Seattle exhibited his work in a one-man show. He has been published in *Smithsonian*.

C. Fred Zeillemaker began seriously photographing birds while in the Navy. He has served with the U.S. Fish and Wildlife Service in refuges across the country.

Guenter Ziesler has photographed the wildlife of South America, the Galapagos, New Guinea, Africa, and India, as well as his native Europe. He is the author of *Safari: The East African Diaries of a Wildlife Photographer*.

Dale and Marian Zimmerman began photographing natural history subjects in the 1940s. Their work appeared in *The Audubon Society Master Guide to Birding*.

Tim Zurowski does most of his photographing from his kayak. He specializes in bird photography, and he has traveled extensively in North America for his pictures.

Index

Numbers in italics indicate pictures